WOZA AFRICA!

DOUGLAS KIRKLAND

COME ON AFRICA!

COME ON
WOZA

AFRICA!

Music goes to War

Foreword by Nelson Mandela
Text by Kole Omotoso

Jonathan Ball Publishers
Johannesburg

All rights reserved.
No part of this publication may be reproduced or transmitted,
in any form or by any means, without prior permission from the publisher
and the copyright holder

©International Committee of the Red Cross (ICRC), Geneva, 1997

Published by
JONATHAN BALL PUBLISHERS (PTY) LTD
PO Box 33977
Jeppestown 2043

ISBN 1 86842 059 0

Art Director: Michael Rand, London
Designer: Ian Denning, London
Photographic co-ordinator: Suzanne Hodgart, London
Editor: Paul-Henri Arni (ICRC), Geneva
Assistant Editor: Yacine Sar (ICRC), Geneva

Colour reproduced by Graphic Facilities, London
Printed and bound by National Book Printers, Drukkery Street,
Goodwood, Western Cape

Contents

6 Foreword by Nelson Mandela

10 Musicians with a message

24 War in modern Africa

44 War zones through the eyes of the musicians

70 What needs to be done

Musicians with a mission

In 1996 five leading African musicians, Youssou N'Dour, Papa Wemba, Jabu Khanyile of Bayete, Lagbaja and Lourdes Van-Dunem undertook an epic journey through some of Africa's most desperate war zones: Liberia, the Sudan-Kenya border, Angola and KwaZulu-Natal, where they were hosted by Africa's reggae superstar Lucky Dube. As a result they recorded *So Why?*, an emotional collective song appealing for reconciliation in Africa. This powerful call was first made public at a live concert in Paris in April 1997, pictured above. A campaign for greater respect for civilians in war is being launched in Africa in 1997 through a record, a documentary film and this book.

Foreword by Nelson Mandela

"I join these musicians…"

In centuries of struggle against racial domination, South Africans of all colours and backgrounds proclaimed freedom and justice as their unquenchable aspiration. They pledged loyalty to a country which belongs to all who live in it. Those who sought their own freedom in the domination of others were doomed in time to ignominious failure.

Out of such experience was born the understanding that there could be no lasting peace, no lasting security, no prosperity in

Shortly after his release from prison, Nelson Mandela in Soweto, South Africa; June 1990.
Photograph by Annie Leibovitz

this land unless all enjoyed freedom and justice as equals, as well as the vision of a free South Africa, of a nation united in diversity and working together to build a better life for all. Our nation emerged from the darkest night into the bright dawn of freedom and democracy.

To the extent that the entire continent of Africa took active part in liberating her southern-most tip, to that extent can the continent as a whole – free at last – join hands in pursuit of her rennaissance. Among other challenges, this means giving free reign to her people's intellectual, cultural, economic and political enterprise. It means creating an environment in which democracy, tolerance, human rights and justice find expression under the African sun. It means ridding the continent of internecine conflict wherever it rears its ugly head; and ensuring that Africa's children can play with gay abandon in the knowledge that their future is secure.

I commend this initiative of the International Committee of the Red Cross to promote Africa's rebirth as a vibrant, peaceful and prosperous continent. I join these musicians in appealing to all Africans to make Africa a continent of our dreams.

Nelson Mandela
President
Republic of South Africa
August 1997

The Paris Concert

The musicians on stage at Le Parc de la Villette performing *So Why?*, a powerful collective song calling for reconciliation and respect for civilians in today's wars in Africa.

Photograph by Douglas Kirkland

Musicians with a message

PAUL GRABHORN

Musician with a message

Papa Wemba
Democratic Republic of Congo

Papa Wemba is the most popular singer in the Democratic Republic of Congo and his popularity extends to Western and Central Africa as well as Southern Africa. He is also well known in France, Belgium, Switzerland and Germany. His last international album *Emotion*, released by Peter Gabriel on his *Real World* label in 1995, has brought him world-wide fame with concerts taking place in Japan, Europe and thirteen African countries in 1996. Papa Wemba is the acknowledged leader of the rich Congolese musical scene. In September 1996 in Johannesburg he shared with his friend Youssou N'Dour the Award for Best African Artist at the KORA, the first all-Africa Music Awards. Papa Wemba brings to the team of musicians a deep emotional inspiration grounded in maturity. He has a wonderful way with children.
Photograph by Douglas Kirkland

Musician with a message

Lagbaja
Nigeria

Lagbaja is a young Nigerian musical genius whose roots are deeply planted in the Nigerian tradition of highlife. He performs dressed in traditionally woven cloth masks, a choice aimed at speaking for the common suffering, anonymous being of Africa. A musician without a face speaking for people without a voice. This fits perfectly with this campaign and through him the voiceless and faceless victims of war speak out their plea to the rest of the world. Lagbaja's second album was released in March 1996 by *Sony Nigeria*, and immediately hit the top of the Nigerian charts. Besides being a composer, performer and producer, Lagbaja is also a stunning saxophonist.
Photograph by Douglas Kirkland

Musician with a message

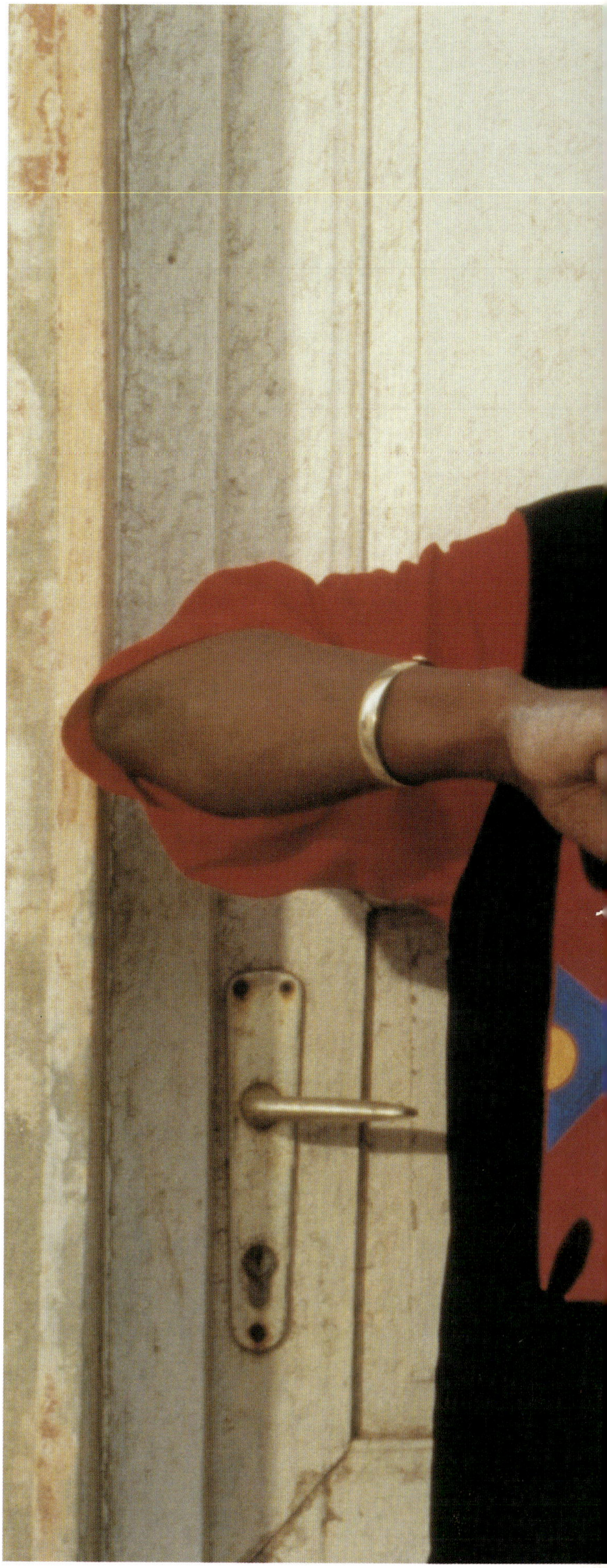

Jabu Khanyile of Bayete
South Africa

In Zulu, Bayete means Majesty, a royal salute. When Jabu Khanyile came up with *Mmalo-We* he started a fire in South Africa. This single reached the ears of Chris Blackwell from *Island Records* who released Bayete's disc on his world music label *Mango*. The album went platinum in South Africa and climaxed in 1994 with a fistful of SAMAs (South Africa Music Awards) – Best Male performer of the year and Best Producer. In July 1996, he performed with his band in London at the Prince of Wales Trust for disabled children. In September 1996 at the first all-Africa Music Awards, he won the KORA for Best Southern African Artist.

Jabu Khanyile, born in Soweto, is a great musician whose inspiration, shared with Lucky Dube, is deeply rooted in Zulu traditions and whose world music style is very powerful. On stage, with his characteristic fly whisk, he captures everyone's heart with his infectious joy and energy.
Photograph by Douglas Kirkland

Musician with a message

Lourdes Van-Dunem
Angola

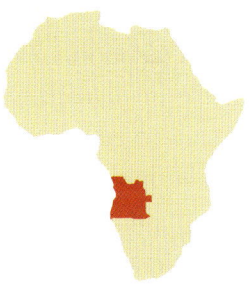

Lourdes Van-Dunem is the great Lady of Angolan music and in many ways she is comparable to Cesaria Evora, the moving singer from Cape Verde. Lourdes's personal fate is linked to the fate of Angola: 20 years of war has given her no chance to record, but has made her a singer with strong messages and a powerful energy. Today a fragile peace in her ravaged country gives her the chance to tell the world what war does to people and how peace should be cherished and protected. The style of her music is typically Angolan: fast, rhythmic and salsa-oriented. In 1996 in Lisbon she recorded and released her first album in many years.
Photograph by Douglas Kirkland

Musician with a message

Youssou N'Dour
Senegal

Youssou N'Dour is one of the most famous contemporary African musicians. He achieved international stardom in 1994 with the hit single *7 Seconds* (a duet with Neneh Cherry) which reached number 2 in America and number 1 in eight European countries. In September 1996 he shared with Papa Wemba the Award for Best African Artist at the KORA, the first all-Africa Music Awards in Johannesburg. In March 1997, he entered a recording studio in New York to record his next international album. Youssou N'Dour has a fantastic capacity to get messages across and to mobilize people for a cause through his music. In Senegal he has reached an extraordinary popularity ranging from the ghettoes to the President. His impact on people can be compared to what the Beatles achieved in Europe in the sixties.
Photograph by Douglas Kirkland

Rwandan orphans crowd towards a soldier from the then rebel Rwandan Patriotic Front, May 1994.
Photograph by James Nachtwey

War in modern Africa

What is happening in Africa? Why are signs of positive gains being overwhelmed by tragedies of sisters and brothers killing one another? Why are children being wasted and men, women and the aged turned into heaps of corpses and stragglers on refugee routes through the forests and valleys of Africa? Surely, something is wrong with our continent. If it is true that "African people did not hear of culture for the first time from Europeans; that their societies were not mindless but frequently had a philosophy of great depth and beauty… they had dignity",[1] I must wonder what is happening today. Europeans themselves acknowledge that African societies did have philosophies and cultures and dignity and they too are bewildered by what is happening in Africa. Where now is the African

Somalia, 1992: famine fuelled by war killed some 300,000 people. A dead child being wrapped in a Red Cross food bag for burial.
Photograph by James Nachtwey

philosophy, where the African culture and the African dignity on which we pride ourselves, to help us out of our present confusion? The most disturbing tragedy is the many civil wars and their effects on unarmed women, children and aged people.

The condition of the victims of war in Africa has become intolerable. That the same can be said for situations of armed conflicts in Europe, Asia or any other parts of the world is, alas, no excuse for the horror that armed conflict has brought to the lives and deaths of Africans. War in Africa has caused not only physical and human damage but also moral and cultural devastation.

> "War has been transformed into butchery and belligerents strike army and civilian population alike without any distinction between the two. However, all abuses lead to a reaction... International conscience demands the condemnation of all these barbarous proceedings. The world is amazed and stunned before these rivers of blood, these hillocks of bones, these mountains of ruins..."[2]

The causes of, and the justifications for, these armed conflicts are not the concern of this ardent and urgent book. Rather, the subject of this book is: what happens when armed conflicts take place in Africa. Ordinary men and women and children are suddenly caught without status in both time and space! From 6am to 6pm, during the hours of the day, the government orders the lives of Mrs. Citizen and her family in one direction. And from 6pm to 6am, during the hours of night and darkness, the rebels requisition her life and the lives of her family in a diametrically opposite direction. What are the moral and cultural implications of displacement in time and space?

Africa is going through a traumatic process of regeneration and renaissance, a process of transformation. If we are not to be lost in the "trance" of this transformation, we must halt the ongoing deadening of moral and cultural sensitivities. We have not been able to avoid warfare in bringing about our renaissance. Yet, it is important to remember that

> "War, so long as it cannot be done away with, must be subjected to ethical and legal controls."[3]

These controls are the signs of a philosophy, a culture and some dignity in any society. If in fact African societies did have a philosophy, a culture and had dignity, they must have evolved controls over the waging of war before the coming of Europeans and other invaders of the continent. There is evidence of such controls in most African societies.

> "You know", he said, "in our tradition, when someone is killed, the tribe of the man who killed him brings a gift called 'sabenhir'. It is the action before the 'diya' – the blood money that is paid for someone's life. It is meant to convince the other tribe that you are ready to apologise. They

An old lady at a feeding centre during the famine resulting from the civil war, Ayod, southern Sudan, 1993.
Photograph by Alexandra Avakian

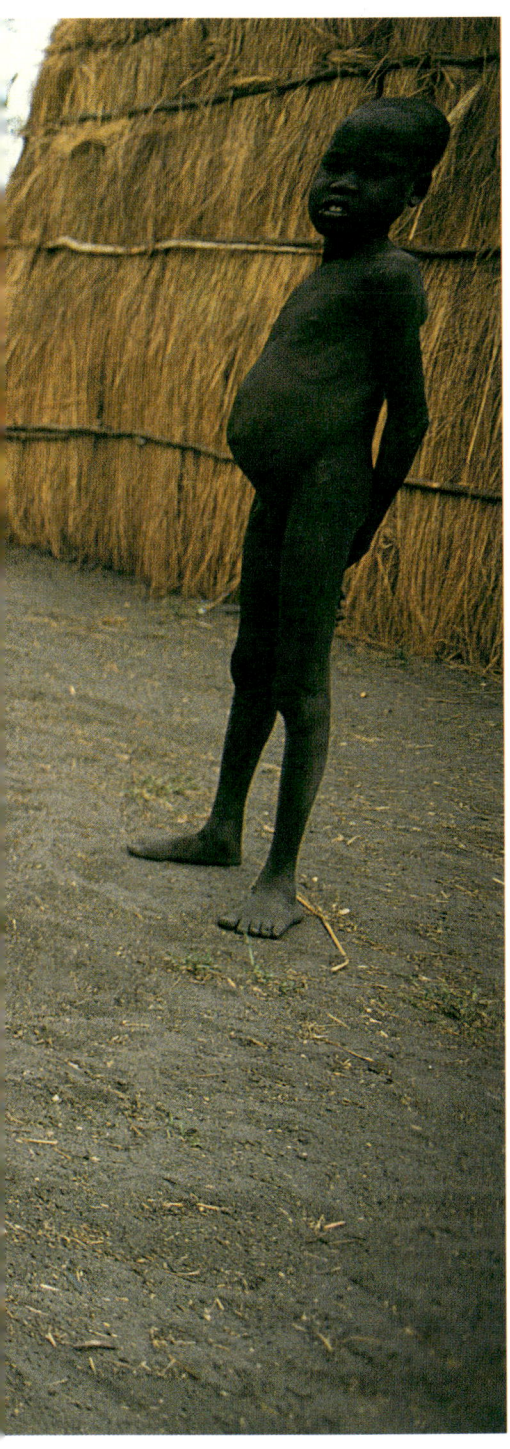

will then arrange a big meeting, then come together and discuss the 'diya'. When the civil war broke out, all traditions had been totally lost and the elders had lost their power."[4]

This book focuses on what happens in war. Research shows that various African societies in the East and West of the continent had rules and regulations governing (1) personal behaviour during armed conflicts; (2) the treatment of defeated enemies and (3) the means of settling conflicts. It should be recognized, though, that differences did exist between the practice of those who lived in the rain forests and that of the societies who lived in the cattle-rearing northern parts of the continent. All the same, there were practices common to all in the conduct of war and the pursuit of peace. One of the most cherished rules had to do with the inviolate position of the elderly, women and children. Age is respected in Africa because the aged have their experience to fall back on and attempt to direct the young. The elderly in Africa have been compared to libraries and their death to the burning of libraries. Armed conflicts in causing the death of the elderly lead to moral and cultural destruction.

Women, the sacred sources of life, were immune from attack during periods of armed conflict.

"Generally, they (women) remained in the village and as fighting was always outside the village, the combatants, in this way, protected the village and the children and old people, or they removed the children and old people to a safe place so that they would not be harmed during the fighting. In Senegal, in the region of Cape Verde, the children and old people were put aboard canoes and taken out to sea."[5]

As in the case of women, children occupy a unique position in the life of Africans. Given the desperation with which men and women seek to have children, it is not surprising that

"Children were the second category of protected persons and were therefore to be spared. Indeed, in all traditional societies of black Africa, a boy became a man only after various initiation ceremonies, including circumcision. Not until such rites had been performed was he considered an adult, no matter what his age. In Africa, as almost everywhere else, a man can only fight and kill another man. As a result, children are kept aloof from fighting."[6]

There were also restrictions on the length of fighting. While some of these observances might have been for the benefit of the belligerent party rather than the vanquished, the fallout was positive for all concerned. Among the Yoruba of West Africa for instance, the Yoruba generalissimo could not wage a war beyond three months without the express permission of the Alafin, the Yoruba king and his council. If after three months he had not brought the fight to a successful conclusion by defeating the enemy, he must commit ritual suicide and his body brought back home. In East Africa, fighting could not go on during the harvesting or the planting season.

There were also restrictions on the "choice of weapons" as well as the "methods of combat". Poisoned arrows and spears were not allowed since the idea was to "strike but not to kill". Ambushes, stabbing in the back and arriving to attack without prior warnings were not permitted.

In spite of these traditional rules of the "war game", it is clear that even when some of Africa's present day warlords do agree to a traditional form of undertaking in the conduct of war or truce, the agreements are not honoured. Here is a too common example:

> "Somalis did not accept the mayhem passively. Religious leaders like Sheik Mohammed Moalim, Sheik Ibrahim Sulay and Sheik Sharafow would clamber across the debris with white flags imploring the militiamen to stop. Siad remembers that these three men also organised a rally of religious leaders which walked between the lines to show the fighters that the carnage was against their own religion and their own people. As the religious demonstration passed, the firing stopped, but when it moved on the fighting began again."[7]

Generally then, the underlying principle, brought out forcefully in the types of games men and boys played, was that an enemy cannot be so totally crushed that he could not continue to have a meaningful existence. Consider the following song:

If all shares are yours
If my share is yours
If your share is yours
Then where is my share?

Dr. Marcel Junod, an ICRC delegate, narrates an experience which he had while he was in Abyssinia (Ethiopia). He had fallen into the hands of armed robbers and was lucky to survive. After a day of hiding he decided to seek help, only to end at the door of one of the armed robbers who had attacked him and his people in the first place. But he was too weak to do anything about it and he went on into the house.

> "I knew that I was saved as soon as I fell over the threshold because, just as in the East, a man mustn't be killed under your roof even if he's your worst enemy."[8]

These then are a few examples of the traditions of warfare in Africa. If all that has happened in Africa today in warfare was merely the idea that

> "In war things which are necessary to attain the end in view are permissible"[9]

An Ibo soldier during the Biafra civil war, Nigeria, 1968.
Photograph by Gilles Caron

it would be understandable. Unfortunately, this has not been the case. There has been unnecessary and gratuitous vandalism, butchery and desecration leading to the mutilation of *mutis* (traditional cure) and the introduction of barbaric traditional rituals. There is enough work for all the world to do simply curbing the unnecessary nastiness of warfare in Africa today.

From the ancient African understanding of the need to protect the weak and succour the poor to the present nastiness of greed for economic and political power is a great gulf caused, as some would want us to believe, by colonisation. The full text of Chinua Achebe's statement at the beginning of this introduction reads:

"As far as I am concerned, the fundamental theme must first be disposed of. This theme – put quite simply is that African peoples did not hear of culture for the first time from Europeans; that their societies were not mindless but frequently had a philosophy of great depth and beauty, that they had poetry and, above all, they had dignity. It is this dignity that many African peoples all but lost in the colonial period, and it is this dignity that they must regain." [10]

Yet, most African countries have been independent for about forty years. Why have many not been able to regain this dignity?

The process of traditional cultural and moral erosion, which began way back in the history of the last five hundred years, accelerated in the second half of the twentieth century. There were various attempts at cultural revival but many of these attempts did not go beyond the change of names from European-sounding to African-sounding ones. African culture became museum items. The fact that we have to seek oral informers to tell us about African rules and regulations on warfare speaks volumes about the situation of African traditional morality. While the old has been eroded, the new humanist morality of the free market has not taken root even among the African elite who have been schooled in these European traditions. This is one of the reasons why we have the present problems caused by armed conflicts in Africa.

A number of African states, which should have inherited the best of both worlds – African and European – have disintegrated. They could no longer fulfil their responsibilities to their citizens. The citizen is then forced to depend on himself/herself and the immediate family, clan and tribe for basic needs such as food, water, clothing and a sense of belonging and some dignity. The strengthening of such natural loyalties spells doom for democracy, which depends on a constant changing of the citizen's mind through the apprehension of new facts or new situations. While the state is disintegrating, groups within the elite arise, promising change if only they can get their hands on state power. This is the beginning of armed disputes for power between the government and the opposition.

The government forces harass the citizen by day and the armed opponents harass him and her by night. The one operates under the safety of daylight from 6 am to 6 pm while the other operates under the conspir-

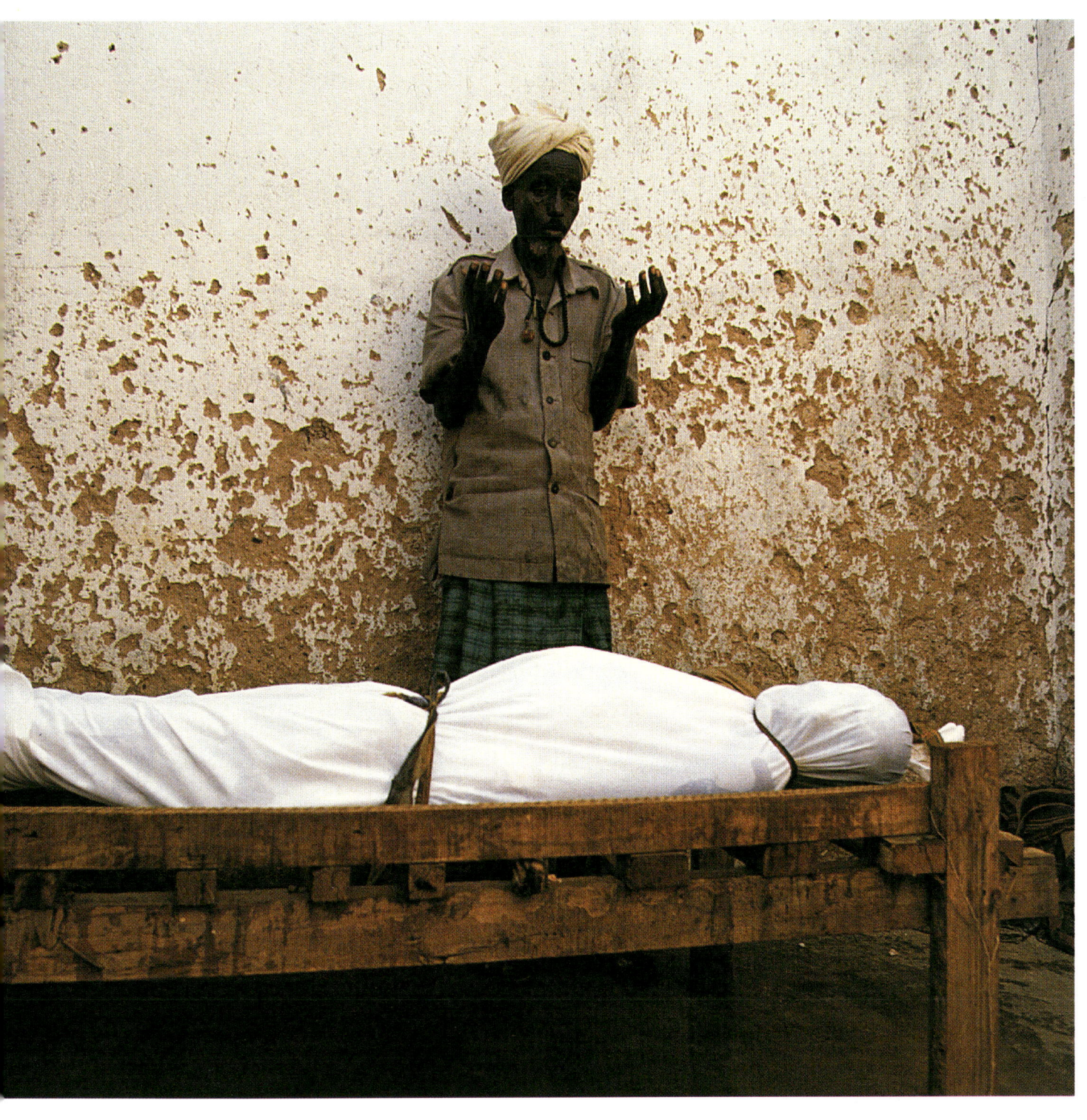

Burial rites for a victim of the civil war in Baidoa, Somalia, 1992.
Photograph by Alexandra Avakian

atorial safety of the night from 6 pm to 6 am.

A family of Father Citizen, Mother Citizen, Sons and Daughters Citizens with their Uncles and Aunts Citizens and their Neighbour Citizens are not cash-rich but they are resource-rich. There was land in abundance and water as well. Exchange took place in the market where items of foreign consumerism could also be purchased.

Mother Citizen had always commented on the way Africa had changed from the time of her own youth. Things were no longer what they used to be. Father Citizen always told her not to judge the present times with the yardstick of the past. But it was true. Things were changing and it was not for the better.

Then real trouble arrived one day. Father Citizen had gone to the farm. Their elder son came from the city to tell them that he was going back to the United States of America where he had found a good job and a place to use his training for the benefit of himself and his fellow citizens. Could he not wait until his father came back from the farm? No. He had to go. He would write to them. He would send them money. The next day their daughter came and said she had got a job in Saudi Arabia as a medical doctor. Although she was not a Muslim, she would bear the rigours of the society rather than die of the frustration of seeing her patients die because there is no oxygen in the hospital. She too promised to keep in touch with them and send money for her brother's and sister's education.

There was no food in the house. One morning the government soldiers arrived and took over the house. It was needed to defend the country against the rebels. They gave Mother Citizen a quarter bag of rice and some cooking oil. They also gave her and her family twenty-four hours to leave the house. That night the rebels called, discovered the food and accused Mother Citizen and her family of taking food bribes from the government in order to betray the revolution. They confiscated the food, assaulted Mother Citizen and abducted Boy Citizen. They could not locate the whereabouts in the house or in the neighbourhood of Daughter Citizen. This was the break up of the Citizen family.

Boy Citizen was turned into Boy Soldier by the end of that traumatic night on the match to the rebel camps. His training included being told that the government was responsible for the problems of his family and that he had to avenge himself. In the morning he got a Kalashnikov AK47 – light enough for a nine-year-old to carry and easy to dismantle and put together again by a child in a few minutes. In the evening Boy Soldier, along with a few others his age, younger or older, was marched back to his village and made to kill their Neighbour Citizen as a way of committing himself to the struggle of the rebels. Could he ever return to that community again, ever? Many of the Boy Soldiers had hernias, perhaps from carrying loads ten times their weight, and there were many eye injuries among them. They were not a particularly healthy lot. What will these children ever know about Africa's traditionally humanitarian ways of treating enemies in war when their fathers and grandfathers, their mothers and grandmothers are dying on crowded roads towards refugee camps all over the continent?

Street killing in Monrovia, Liberia, April 1996. A young fighter is chased, caught and stabbed to death by opponents from another faction. The violence which flared up in April and May 1996 in Monrovia was the fiercest fighting in the country's seven-year civil war that caused the death of over 150,000 people.
Photograph by Corinne Dufka

Overleaf: A starving child in a refugee camp during the famine and civil war, Baidoa, Somalia, 1992.
Photograph by Jean-Claude Coutausse

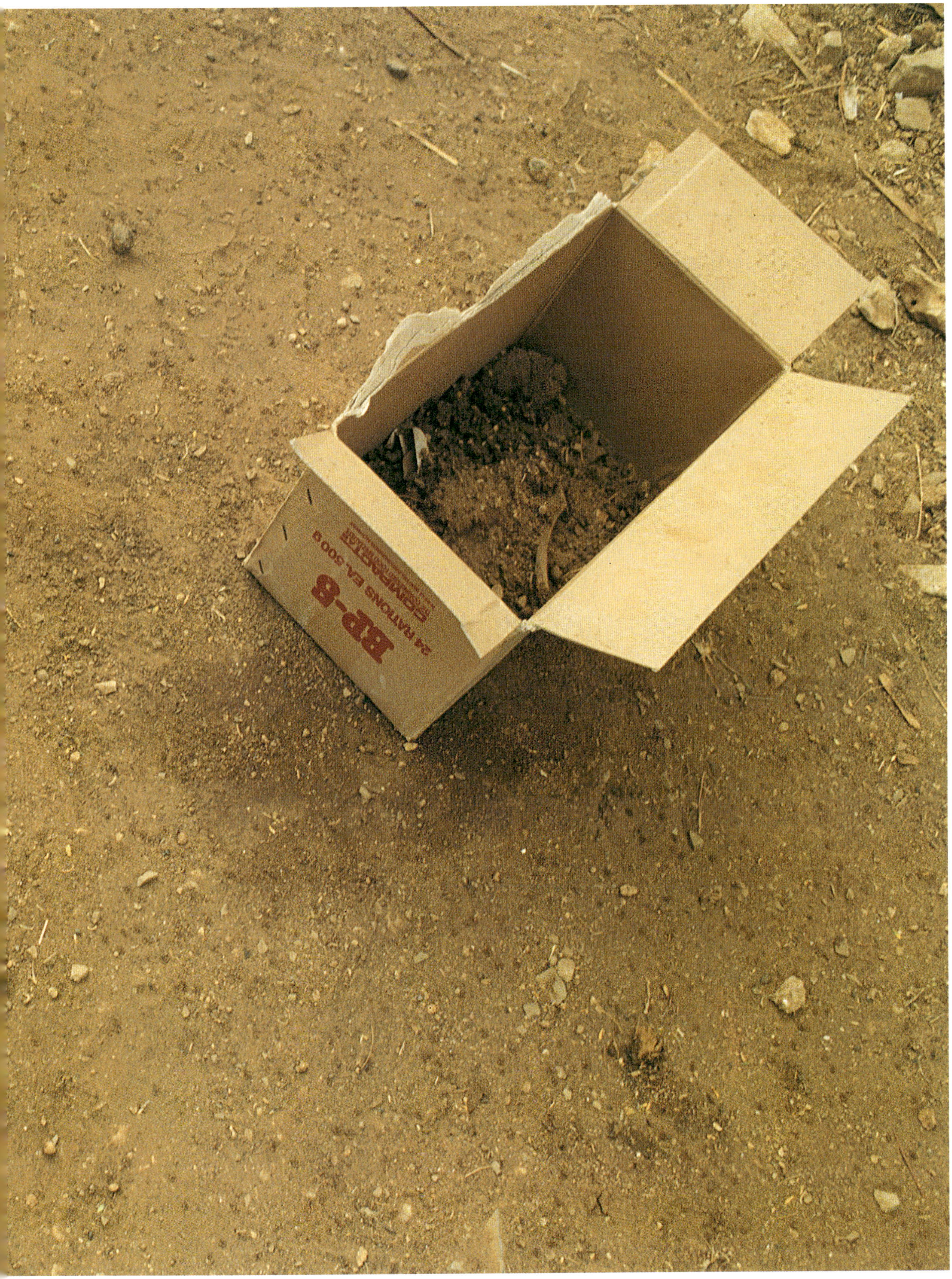
BP-5
24 RATIONS EA. 500 g

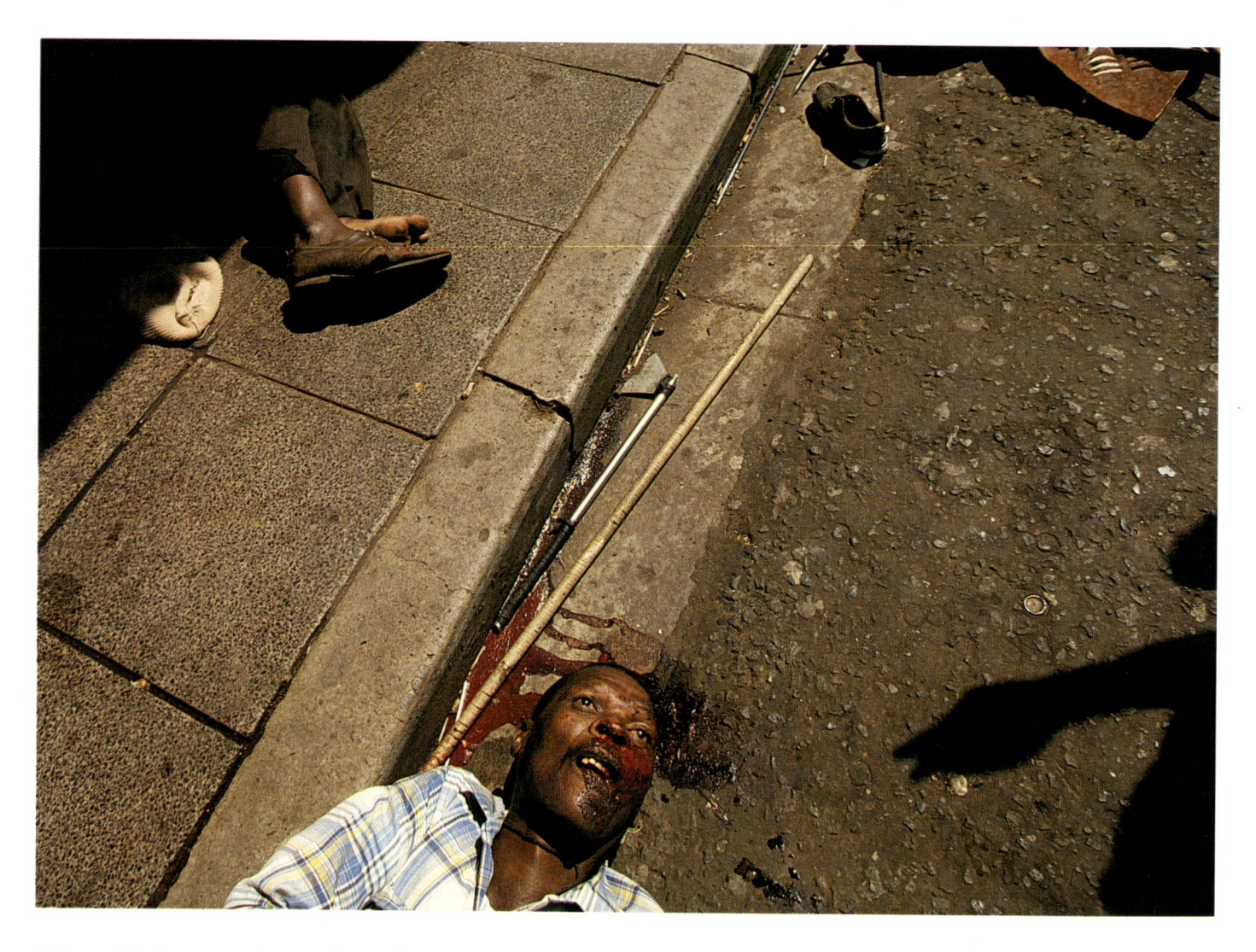

What will they ever know about the Geneva Conventions when they can hardly read, thanks to the breakdown of the school system under the government and the failure of the rebels to set up any infrastructure in the areas they control? Their future is too bleak to leave to contemplation alone. Something needs to be done.

In the meantime, Mother Citizen could think of only one place to go – where her community fetched its water from the communal wells. She did not know where to go, never having been to too many places without her husband. But when she reached the wells, she was told that their former neighbours, now their enemies, had taken them over, fenced them in with barbed wire and put government soldiers there to ensure that nobody else was allowed near the water. Landmines had been planted around the wells, and along the shores of the rivers.

Where do we go from here? Someone said that there was a refugee camp where food and water was available for all those who made it to the camp. By late afternoon when they arrived at the refugee camp, there must have been over a thousand women, children and old people .

Daughter Citizen, like her mother, had escaped from the house and gone on to the wells, only to be captured by the government forces and made to work for them in the kitchen.

Father Citizen found on reaching the farm that he could not harvest

Above: Aftermath of a street battle between supporters of of the Inkhata Freedom Party (IFP) and of the African National Congress (ANC) during the general election campaign. Johannesburg, South Africa, 1994.
Photograph by Tomas Muscionico

Right: A victim of the famine and a soldier at a refugee camp in Kurtum Warey, Somalia, 1992.
Photograph by Jean-Claude Coutausse

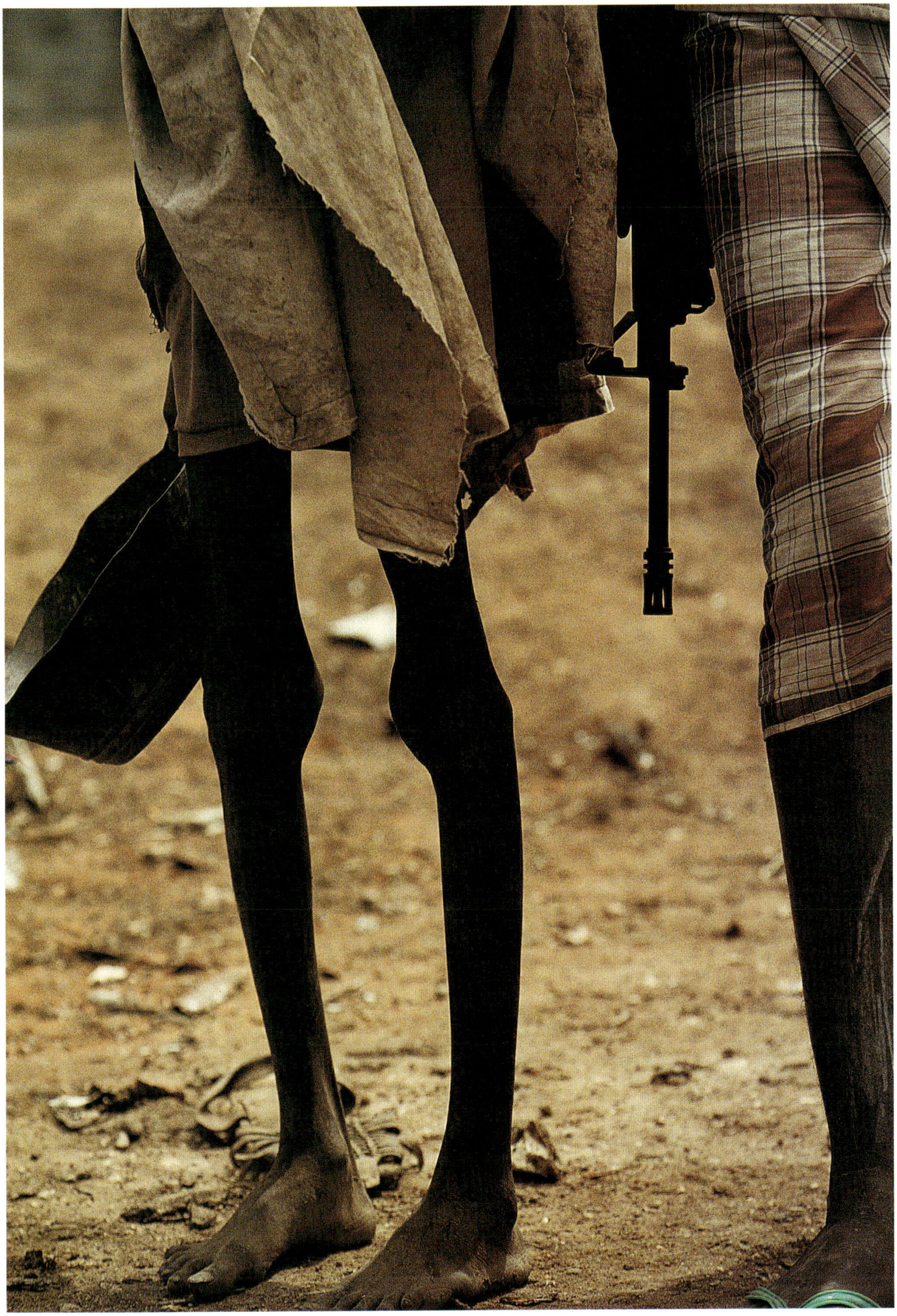

anything because the crops had been looted and landmines planted to prevent him and others like him from coming back to farm the land. He too joined the multitude of refugees but in the opposite direction from his wife.

Stories of mine tragedies circulated among the refugees. There is eleven-year-old Alexander whose father is a sergeant in the government army. Walking to school in the morning, Alexander was asked by his father to come and meet him in his military post after school. In the course of that morning Alexander's father gave orders to the soldiers with him in the government headquarters to plant mines around the office so that rebel soldiers would not surprise them. Not knowing about them, Alexander went to meet his father after school, only to walk over one of the mines planted on his father's order and his right leg was blown off. Why father, why?

There was the prize bull of Father Citizen's neighbour blown up by a landmine. Citizen neighbour was going to use the bull as part of his *lobola* (bride price). The herdboy was also killed by a nearby landmine.

There was the twelve-year-old girl going to the river to fetch water and firewood with her mother and her two legs were blown off and her mother blown to pieces. Why, mother, why? It is under these circumstances that the Women of Africa petitioned the Organisation of African Unity thus:

We, the women of Africa, are hurting.
For thousands, nay, millions of years
We have been mothering this Continent.
We have carried and delivered life, we have nursed it to maturity –
Loving, caring, nursing, teaching –
Through slavery, colonial rule, the struggle for independence.
We have protected the young and nursed the old.
We have participated in resistance to conquest
And outside domination.
We have watched the plunder of resources of our land.
And we have nursed the wounds.
We continue to toil daily at home,
In the farms, markets, factories, offices.
And now, these genocidal wars, wars
That destroy what we have so painstakingly constructed.
The wars have ravaged our children, our bodies, our fragile hands.
The wars have robbed us of our dignity and selfworth.
They have disinherited our children from their land and rendered
  us wanderers
Subjected to hostility, shame, destitution.
They have killed and maimed, decimated our children
And desecrated our shrines.
Worse, they have bloodied our hands,
Made us commit atrocities,
The shame of which we shall never forget.

Is nobody listening?

Rwandan Hutu refugees fleeing a combat zone near the village of Biaro (42 kilometres from Kisangani), former Zaire, March 1997.
Photograph by Sebastião Salgado

It is part of the transformation taking place in Africa today that there is a demographic explosion leading to the existence of 420 million young people below the age of 25 on the continent; that there is the final emergence of a new generation of African businessmen and women, artists and politicians, a true civil society of a middle class able and willing to play the role of creating states on the continent as the post-colonial state suffers disintegration. With the breakdown of the state, and the disregard of national and international law, a group of national and international figures have emerged to whom the continent and the rest of the world would listen. These are the world-famous footballers and athletes, writers and artists and especially musicians. African youth as well as their elders are listening to the musicians of Africa. This is because of the positive roles they have taken on themselves to play in the present process of transformation.

Youssou N'Dour of Senegal is one of these African and international personalities. Working with traditional values, these musicians express the aspirations of their people and address the powerful political leaders of Africa to listen to their peoples.

For some years now, there has been a rebel movement in the Senegalese region of Casamance, the breadbasket of the country, fighting the government of Senegal. Youssou N'Dour decided to do something about it in 1995 on the 27th of December. He organised a huge musical performance in

National day of mourning for the victims of the genocide. Wooden crates contain the remains of 10,000 victims, who are to be buried on Rebero Hill, eight miles from Kigali, Rwanda, 7 April 1995.
Photograph by Sebastião Salgado

which all leading Senegalese musicians and bands performed. Insisting that there was something in the traditional ways of waging war, the musicians, in the words of Youssou N'Dour, called on the elders and the religious leaders to resolve the situation:

One day, I noticed that there were many soldiers
I asked them where they were going.
They told me 'To Casamance'
A few days before
People had arrived carrying their baggages
They told me that they had been chased from Casamance
Sometimes the Devil takes the human form
To pass through peaceful places and upset them
Why must we give the Devil a role here
When we are all one, our blood is the same
We must do everything possible so peace returns to Casamance.
Through the inspiration of our ancestor
We must think of our children
And ensure that peace comes back to Casamance
The family is dispersed
Gone like the wind
In this condition of battles
Whose origin no one knows
A battle without end
Everything must be done to put out this fire
Or else it will be too late
I ask you to unite
Let every tribe unite
It is the only way out
Religious leaders like our grand-parents in times past
You must unite and bring peace back to Casamance.

The performance of the musicians was transmitted live on national television. The impact was like dynamite around the country. Three months later peace-makers brought the government and the opposition movement to a peace meeting and the rebellion in Casamance was brought on a negotiating track. Such is the power of our musicians.

---

1. Chinua Achebe, *The Role of the Writer in a New Nation* in Nigeria Magazine, No. 81, 1964, p.157.
2. Geoffrey Best, *War and Law Since 1945*, Clarendon Press, 1994, p.103.
3. ibid. p.16.
4. James Schofield, *Silent Over Africa – Stories of War and Genocide*, Harper Collins Publishers, London, 1996, p.9.
5. Yolande Diallo, *African Traditions and Humanitarian Law – Similarities and Differences*, an inquiry, ICRC, p.9.
6. ibid. p.7.
7. James Schofield, op. cit. p.15.
8. Dr. Marcel Junod, *Warrior Without Weapons*, Jonathan Cape, London, 1951, ICRC, Geneva, 1982, p.67.
9. Geoffrey Best, op. cit. p.30.
10. Chinua Achebe, op. cit. p.157.

War zones through

the eyes of the musicians

Lagbaja reads Article 3 of the Geneva Conventions to an Ecomog soldier at a military checkpoint in downtown Monrovia, Liberia. Article 3 prohibits at all times mutilation, cruel treatment, torture and executions without previous judgment.
Photograph by Paul Grabhorn

When European powers colonized Africa, they took control of places – mountains, rivers, valleys and coasts – from tribal kings and chiefs, from clan leaders and local warlords and authorities. From the different spheres of European influence colonial powers put together geo-politically defined nation-states. At the Berlin Conference of 1884–85, these nation-states were given internationally recognized boundaries. These newly bounded places evolved in the next half century or so into countries agitating for independence from the colonial powers. These independence struggles succeeded in the 1960s and African countries joined the society of international states taking their seats at the United Nations Organization and its various agencies, signing international treaties and having succession to others entered into during the colonial history of the countries. In 1964–65 the Organization of African Unity ratified, condoned and endorsed the boundaries of African countries which had been agreed upon by the European powers at the Berlin Conference.

When European colonial powers handed over political power at independence to Africans, they did not hand over power to the same class of people from whom their grandfathers and great-grandfathers had taken power, the holders then of what came to be known as traditional African political power. Political power was handed over to a new class of Africans who had evolved through European education, economic activities and political upbringing.

African countries, made up as they are of a multitude of tribes, clans and language groupings at different stages of self-identification against others, constituted fragile political entities. Disputes over access to land, water and other resources led first to military takeovers of governments and then military conflicts for political power. Hence Biafra, Chad, Congo, Ethiopia, Burundi, Sudan, Rwanda, Mozambique, Angola, Somalia and South Africa.

War came to Africa with new weapons and new objectives and no rules or regulations.

The International Committee of the Red Cross came into Africa at the very beginning of the twentieth century to alleviate the conditions of the victims of the Anglo-Boer War of 1898–1902. But with the almost total erosion of respect for victims of war and basic rules of behaviour in combat in recent conflicts such as Liberia, Rwanda and Burundi, it became almost impossible for humanitarian organizations to do their work successfully. Entire regions became no-go areas. Relief teams came under fire, often being targeted on purpose. The result was entire populations left on their own. Tens of thousands of refugees, displaced persons, maimed and wounded men and women and children remained unattended. In the face of this chaos and human suffering, it was necessary to appeal directly to Africans to look at their situation.

But whom can anyone concerned about the plight of ordinary Africans get to speak to the powerful men and women of Africa? To whom would Africans, high and low, listen? Who can speak of the sufferings of Africa to Africans?

African musicians have made their reputations with chart-topping songs not only in their own countries but also in other African countries and the countries of the world. They have performed throughout Africa, Europe, North and South America and the Caribbean before hundreds of thousands of music lovers. They have made songs to alleviate hunger, fight AIDS and secure the release of Nelson Mandela from prison. African musicians would go to speak to African political leaders on behalf of African peoples.

In the early months of 1996 five African musicians undertook an epic journey in the tradition of hunter-heroes seeking a remedy for communal ailments. These modern-day singer-heroes visited some of Africa's most desperate war zones: Liberia, the Sudan-Kenya border, Angola and KwaZulu-Natal. The rapport of the musicians was very strong, based as it was on their commitment to "educate and entertain", in the words of Lucky Dube. Jabu Khanyile and Lucky Dube had previously worked together for AIDS awareness and other charity performances. Youssou N'Dour and Papa Wemba are

A girl under the protection of a Red Cross flag. The flag has been erected at this abandoned school building to indicate a temporary first-aid clinic that the International Committee of the Red Cross has set up for the day to provide emergency treatment to refugees from the fighting in this area of Burundi.
Photograph by Paul Grabhorn

47

Child soldiers at rebel headquarters,
Tubmanburg, Liberia, 1996.
Photograph by Guenay Ulutunçok

friends going back many years. Lucky Dube and Papa Wemba found themselves playing together, Lucky on piano and Papa on vocals.

The variety and number of people the musicians encountered during these epic journeys were unforgettable.

There was Lola in Huambo in Angola, a widow with three children. Her husband, a soldier, had been killed in an ambush in 1992. The devastating 55-day war virtually started in her bullet-ridden flat in the middle of Huambo. Holed up here where there was some food, she and her neighbours would send out the children to go and fetch water. Three of these children and a women were killed in these forays for life-sustaining water.

There were the encounters with two commanders, one each from both sides of the conflict. Both men would normally have been colleagues and even perhaps friends in a different situation. Here they were facing delicate problems of dealing with their fellow citizens who had been displaced by the struggles in which they were involved. What a waste!

In a unique situation where music comes from various traditions, Jabu Khanyile sings of healing accompanied by one of the refugees on the Sudan-Kenya border playing a traditional Sudanese string instrument. Lagbaja plays a sonorous saxophone while Van-Dunem interprets their music in the measured step of a dance.

In KwaZulu-Natal Lourdes Van-Dunem sings to the widows of violence about the suffering of women and children in wars fought by men. Why must women and children suffer for what they know little about?

Kuito must be the most ravaged town in Africa today. All along the main street beautiful edifices have been reduced to mere shells of bricks perforated with different sizes of bullets and shells. In what used to be the Opera House with its light green painting only a mere remembrance now, Papa Wemba sings deploring such vandalism and wondering what is the purpose of all this self-destruction? Holding a baby girl, one of the orphans of this madness, Papa Wemba sings a lullaby to her, consoling her and hoping that all she would know in the future is the caring attention of fellow human beings rather than the destructive attention which has left her without her natural parents. He is almost in tears as he brushes his lips against the cheeks of the little girl.

In a burnt-out house in KwaZulu-Natal, Lucky Dube rubs off the smoke and ash from a familiar family wish – *May God bless this house and protect all those who live in it*. Why would anyone make such a simple wish impossible?

Angola's minefields are terrible. In a horrendous reversal of what traditionally should be expected, thunder coming with fire and lightning from the skies, it now comes from the earth from planted seeds of destruction. Lourdes Van-Dunem and Jabu Khanyile walk through these killing fields as bewildered as the victims they have encountered.

Children are not only victims, they are also part of the instruments of creating victims. It would even seem that child soldiers are more destructive of life and material because, according to those who have studied the phenomenon, they are "more obedient, do not question orders and are easier

An emotional moment for the musicians as they listen to the lecture on conditions endured by prisoners at the Slave House on Gorée Island, Senegal. Gorée was the main transit point in Africa for millions of slaves deported to the Americas.
Photograph by Paul Grabhorn

51

to manipulate than adult soldiers"! Yet it is common knowledge that

> "no peace treaty to date has formally recognized the existence of child combatants. As a result their special needs are unlikely to be taken into account."[11]

Where is the process that re-integrates a twelve-year-old turned sixteen with a newly acquired assertiveness and independence? What about the girl soldier who has been raped and sexually abused? What roles can these traumatised adults of tomorrow play in the African renaissance we all talk about? What programmes can restore to these youths the treasures of traditional African societies? What rituals can be performed for them to ensure re-entry into their communities? No wonder Papa Wemba's anger as he contemplated the face of a child soldier who seemed to revel in his situation. One of the most pathetic examples of child-soldiering is the Liberian former war criminal who has given himself the name O.J. He began to fight at the age of twelve and continued until he was sixteen in the notorious SBUs (Small Boy Units). O.J. joined the war at the beginning, in 1990, because he was hungry and felt the need for protection. One day, as he was looking for food at Monrovia harbour, he was shot in the left knee by militiamen who were harassing and looting the property of civilians. Soon

Above: Mr Joseph N'Diaye, the Director of the Slave House Museum on Gorée Island, Senegal, describes how weighted chains were used to prevent prisoners from jumping from slave ships on departure from Gorée.

Right: Jabu Khanyile comforts a wounded child in Lokichokio, Northern Kenya, at the ICRC war surgery hospital, the biggest of its kind in the world, where the Red Cross conducts non-stop war surgery for victims of the fighting in southern Sudan.
Photographs by Paul Grabhorn

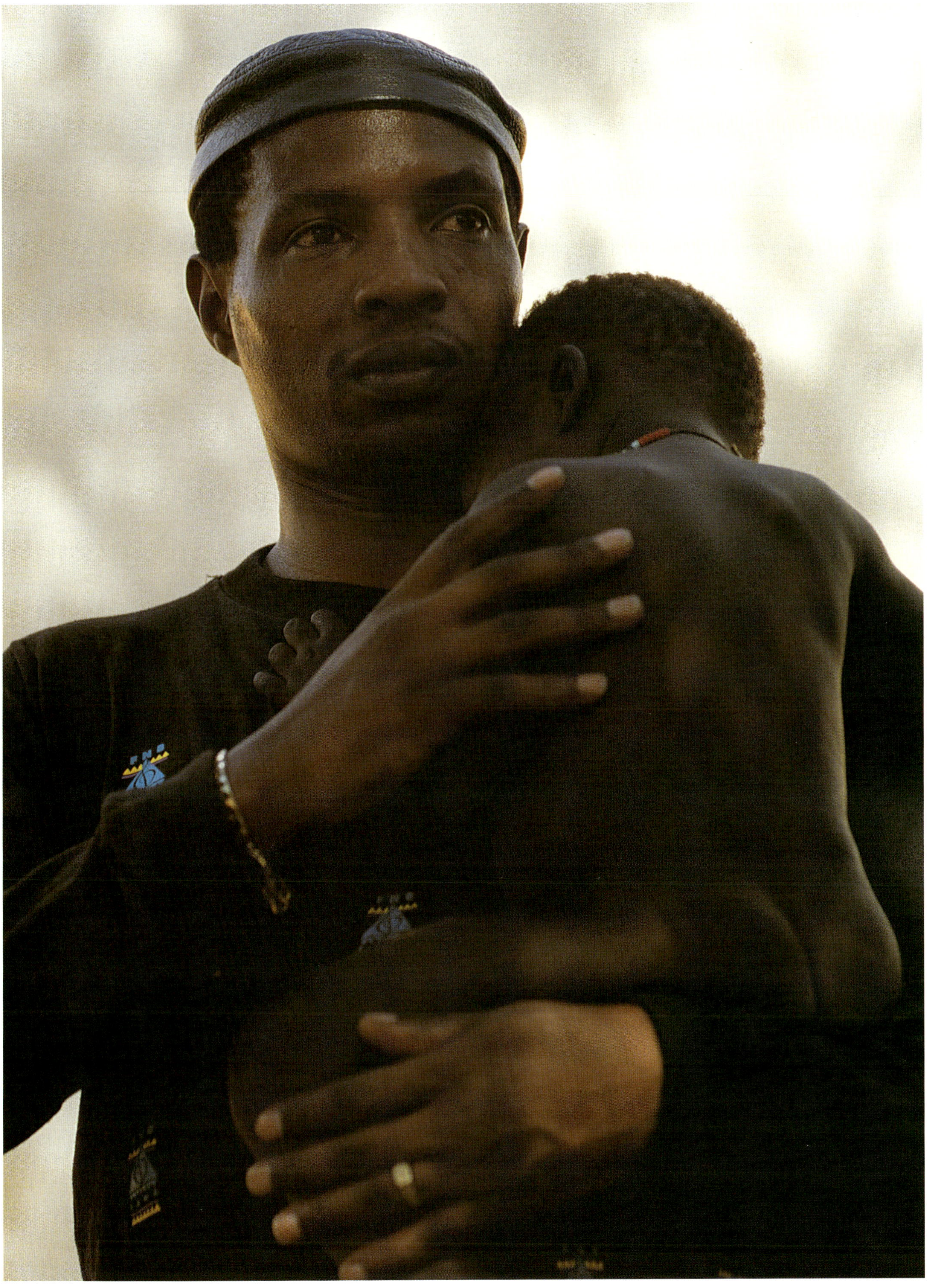

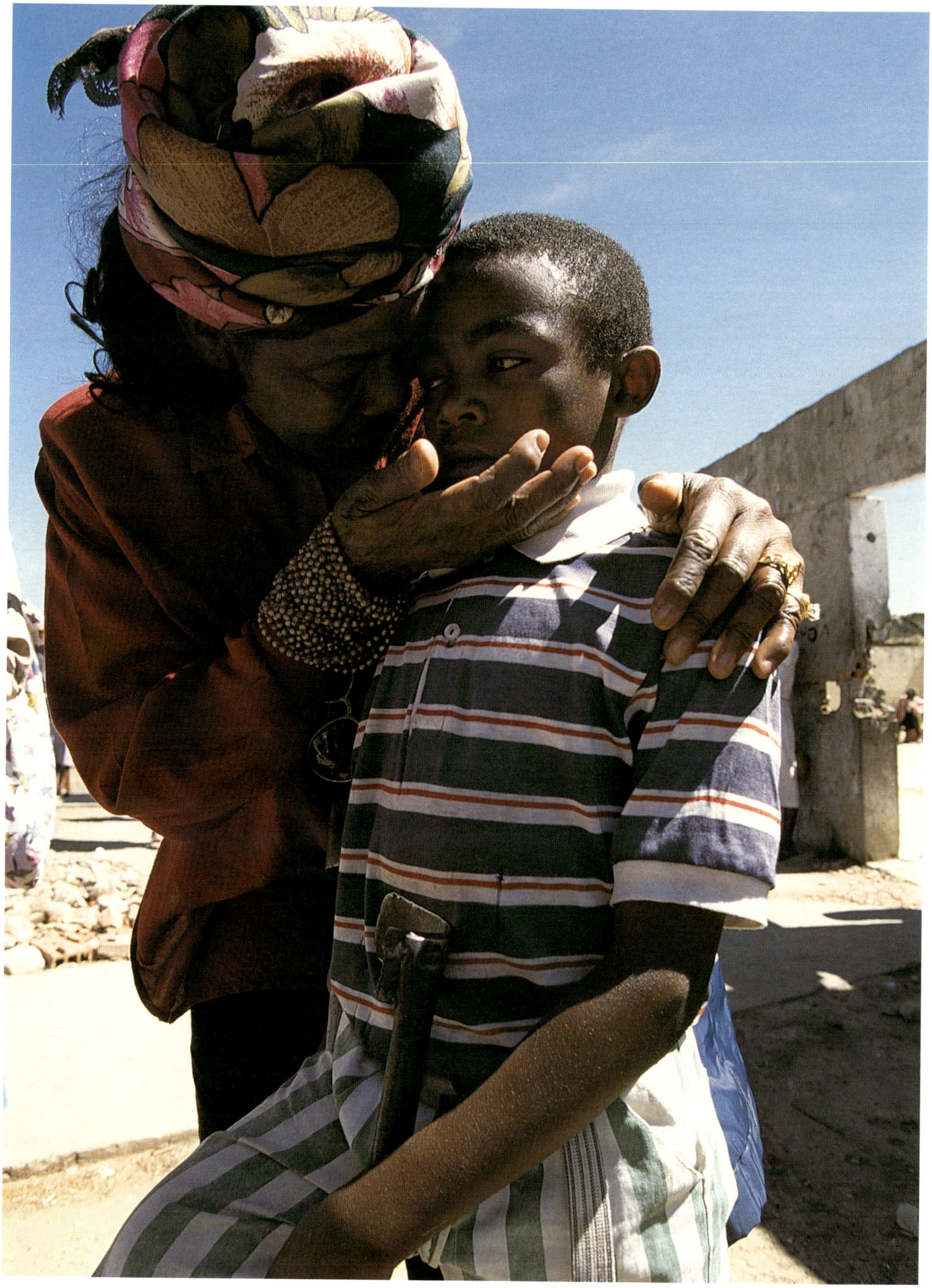

Left: Lourdes Van-Dunem comforts Alexander, an 11-year-old mine victim in Kuito, Angola. This boy lost his right leg when he stepped on a landmine laid by his own father, a soldier.

Above: Lourdes talks with prisoners in Huambo jail, Angola.
Photographs by Paul Grabhorn

afterwards he joined a rebel army, "just to survive", he says. O.J.'s SBU was composed of two other boys aged twelve like himself. As in all other SBUs in this militia, the policy was that these children were on their own, without a leader. He received no military training, just an AK47. His first task was to take a strategic bridge in Monrovia. A bullet wounded him in the head, the scar of which he still bears. He was sent back to base for treatment. One day, as he was recovering, he was told to execute two prisoners with a knife because it was believed that the two prisoners were protected against bullets by magic. O.J. carried out this order without hesitation, cutting the throats of the two prisoners. He was twelve years old.

Killing was not difficult for O.J. and his companions because they were on drugs – everyday for two years. He used to smoke a big joint in the morning, a second at noon and the third in the evening. Sometimes they added to this a "blue pill" (most probably an amphetamine). Then they were so stoned that they were ready for anything. He cannot remember the details of what they did. He knows though that he killed many people himself, "not on orders, just for fun". How many? "I can't count, just many… We did terrible things: we raped countless numbers of women, we tied people up and threw them into the harbour."

From 1992 to 1993 he joined another, better-structured rebel force. His

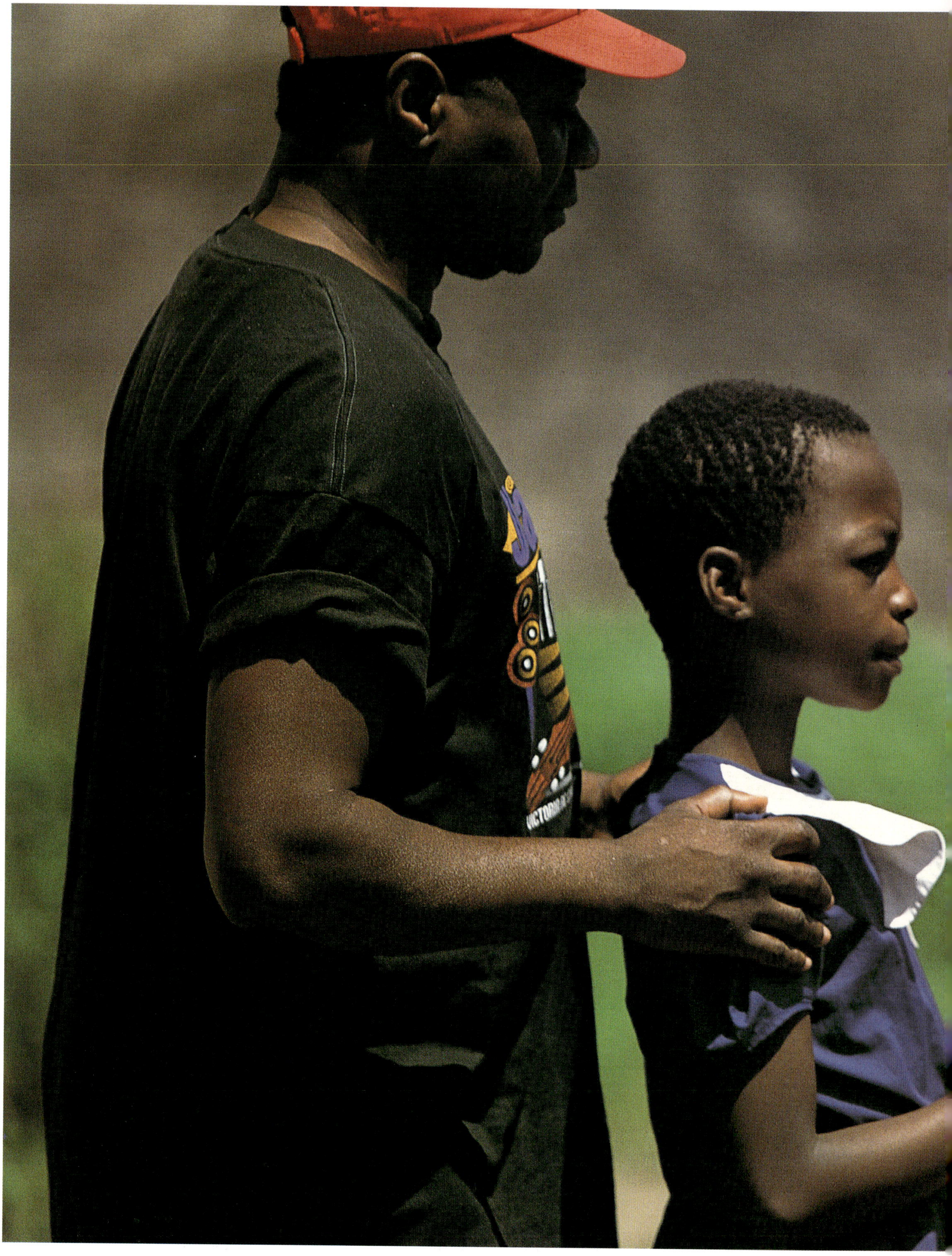

unit was called Alligator Battalion. The misconduct continued, mainly harassing villagers for food. At the end of 1993 he ran away. In 1994 he came to Don Bosco, an Irish NGO which takes care of a few hundred kids orphans, former war victims, former child soldiers as well as former child prostitutes. At night O.J. wanders the streets. He sleeps in Don Bosco shelter on Benson Street where two dreams haunt him: in one he is trying to sleep when men come to him with big knives to kill him. He shouts for help and that's when he wakes up in terror. In the second dream he is the richest man on earth only to wake up to see that he had nothing. The past haunts him while the future is out of his reach.

The war in southern Sudan has gone on for more than ten years now. It is a war that belongs to another age. The conflict has had devastating consequences and has forced hundreds of thousands of people to flee their homes. The country is in ruins and the population has been deprived of its basic means of subsistence. There are no seeds, no tools, no food supplies left. Many villages have been destroyed, and the livestock has been decimated. People flee to escape the fighting, or simply to survive. It sometimes takes these tall-standing nomads almost two months to make their way, slowly and painfully, across the vast expanses of southern Sudan in order to find refuge in neighbouring countries. Many of these people are wounded. A complex air rescue operation fetches the wounded wherever they can be sighted and fly them to Lokichokio hospital which is now the largest Red Cross facility for treating war casualties in the world.

Lokichokio is situated in the bush, about 20 kilometres from the Sudan border. The hospital has 500 beds, with several surgical teams sent out mainly for performing amputations and operations on bullet wounds. It also has an orthopaedic centre, where amputees are fitted with artificial limbs and are taught how to use them. As soon as they are able to walk again, they are flown back to their home villages in southern Sudan. When amputees are issued with artificial limbs they are given shoes to use with the limbs, usually made of canvas. The musicians were told that some of the

Papa Wemba comforts a young girl who has been telling how she saw people killed in front of her during the "Christmas Day massacre" at Shobashobane in KwaZulu-Natal, a province of South Africa, where over 20,000 people have been killed in political violence since 1985.
Photograph by Paul Grabhorn

Overleaf: Papa Wemba sings his heart out on the bullet-pocked stage of an abandoned cinema in Kuito, Angola.
Photograph by Paul Grabhorn

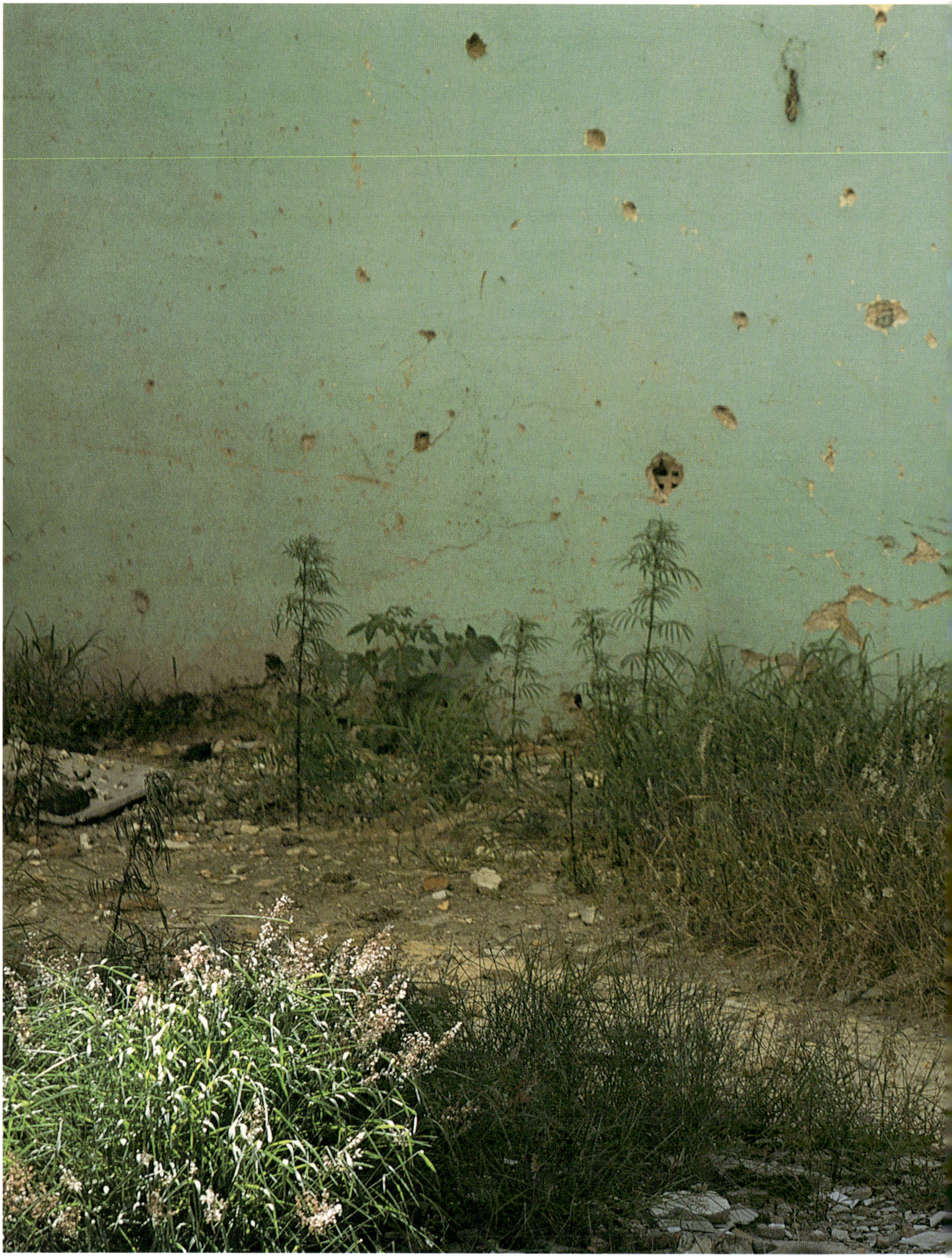

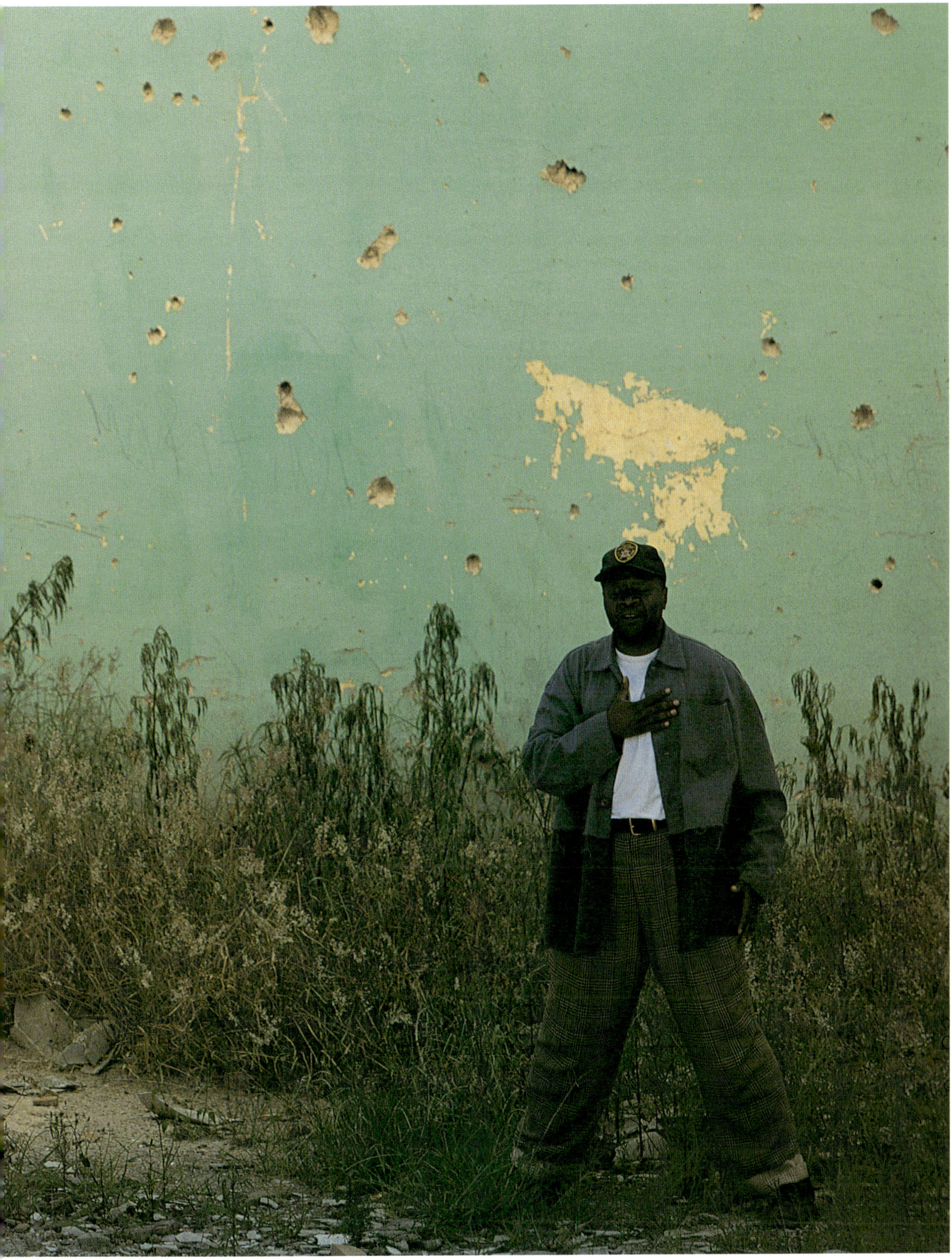

Lucky Dube

Lucky Dube of South Africa was the musicians' host while they were in KwaZulu-Natal in South Africa. Lucky Dube is unique in the musical history of South Africa. In his country, he is the most successful recording artist ever: his album *Prisoner* sold 400,000 copies in South Africa and 600,000 world-wide. His last album *Trinity*, released in 1995, sold over 750,000 copies in the first year according to official Billboard USA charts and sales.

Lucky Dube is Africa's reggae superstar. He has performed all over the world and raises crowds wherever he goes. In the struggle against apartheid, he was one of the most articulate and powerful voices. Today, in countries such as Rwanda, Liberia and Sierra Leone, he represents the ultimate role model for thousands of young and destitute Africans. In this project, he has been the host of the musicians in his home province of KwaZulu-Natal, interviewing victims of political violence in the province and explaining to his fellow artists the complexity of violence-stricken Zululand. He impressed everyone he met with his balanced views. His worldwide commitment did not allow him to participate in the recording of *So Why?* Nevertheless he has contributed a song for the album and is featured in the documentary film of the campaign.
Photographs by Paul Grabhorn

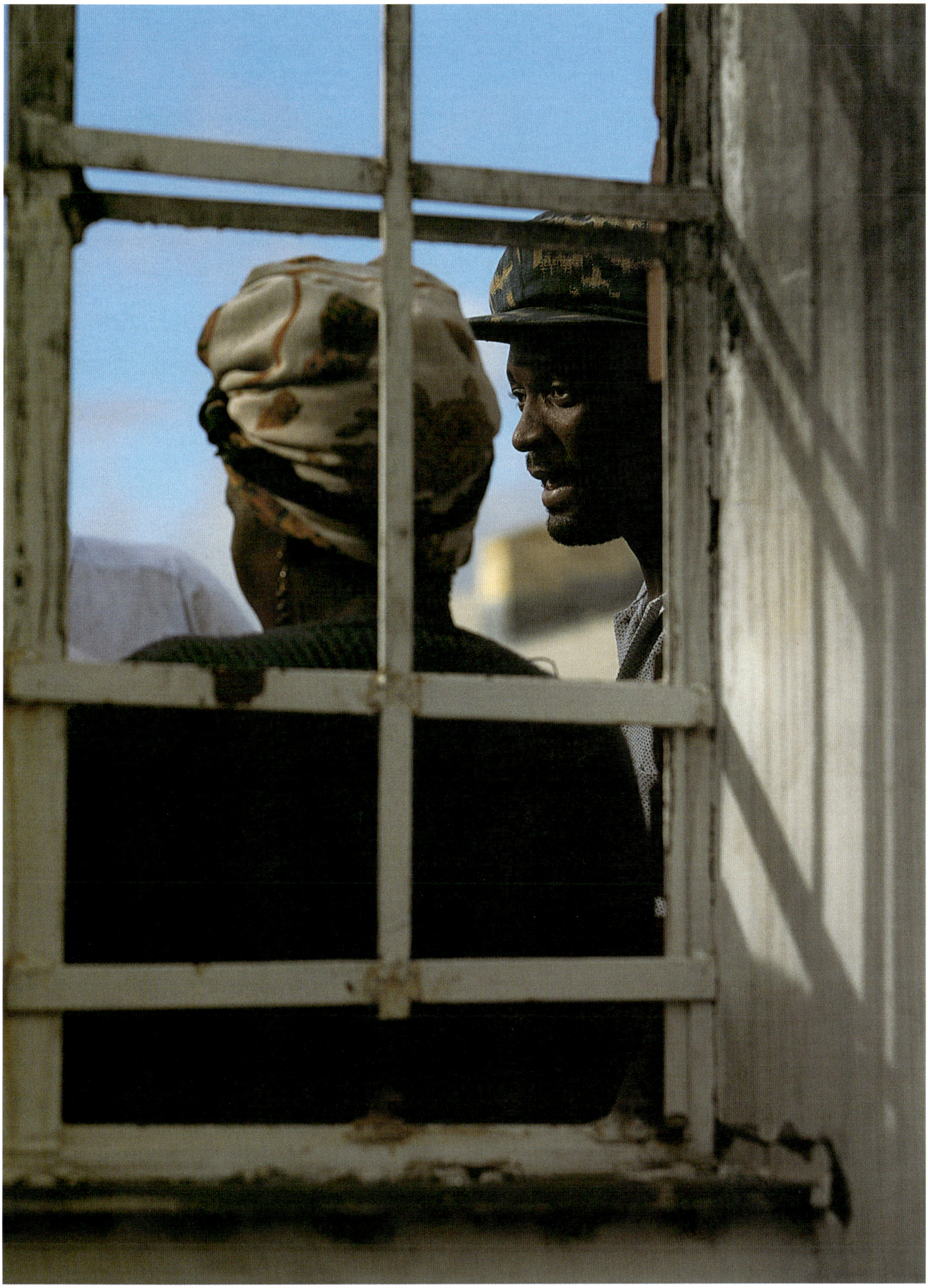

men would use their artificial limbs only on special occasions so as not to wear out their shoes.

Most of these people are farmers. The land cultivated for years suddenly becomes devastated. In an instant their lives are ruined. They are forced to feed the different groups of fighters. Then they are punished for doing so by the opposite side. So they are doubly victimised. They are robbed, bombed, wounded, and driven from their homes. At that point the country's entire food chain collapses.

While all the musicians were affected by everything they saw, each one seemed to have been particularly struck by a specific aspect of the devastation they were seeing in these war zones. For Papa Wemba it was the plight of the children. For Lourdes Van-Dunem it is natural that she would be drawn to share the loss and trauma of the women. Lagbaja was angry about the bad leadership which had made this mayhem possible, while Youssou N'Dour believed that musicians had a responsibility to help with the process of restoration needed in the community. Jabu Khanyile was dismayed by the landmines and Lucky Dube was emphatic that suffering belonged to no party. All suffer in this madness.

The Don Bosco Orphanage is located on the outskirts of Monrovia. Here there are about one hundred and fifty children in different stages of war injury and trauma. Here some workshops have been set up to help the process of re-integration of the child soldiers in the rest of society. It was here that the musicians had one of their most moving jam sessions playing with some of the victims of war. Olas, on the drums, is now twenty-one. He had joined the fighting in Buchanan when he was fifteen in 1990. When war broke out, he and his family took refuge in the bush but they had no food. Olas and his brother went back to town to look for food. One day his brother was caught and executed. Olas was offered a chance to join the militia. He went through a full six-month military training course that included survival and escape techniques. Olas was promoted to lieutenant, though still fifteen. His unit, the First Infantry Battalion, was ordered to attack Monrovia. Their attack failed and they retreated to Buchanan where Olas was assigned to a check-point. It was here that he recognised his brother's murderer, who also recognised him and shot at him. Olas shot back in self-defence and killed him. In 1991 he became deputy commander of his unit. Olas saw children killing people, cutting off fingers, breasts, heads right on the road. He ran away from the war and came to Don Bosco.

John, who plays the bass guitar, lost his two legs, his father and his small sister in one of the worst massacres of the war in Liberia.

The Don Bosco Band was made up of six kids from the orphanage. They were given instruments and they practised everyday. Their most famous song has been released and it was played on national radio. It is called *Drop Your Guns and Go to School* and was a powerful appeal to the 6,000-odd child soldiers in hiding in the Liberian bush. They have another song called *Stop the War!*

The band's favourite singer is Lucky Dube, and they play his songs quite often and quite well, particularly *Prisoner*.

Youssou N'Dour sits on a huge
1907 Navy gun turret, now abandoned,
on Gorée Island, Senegal.
Photograph by Paul Grabhorn

It was with this band that the musicians had an exhilarating jam session, with Lagbaja on saxophone, John, the amputee, on bass guitar, Olas on drums, and Youssou N'Dour, Papa Wemba and Lourdes Van-Dunem at the microphone belting out *Stop the War!*:

Have your minds gone astray?
Have your hearts all gone upset?
Have you closed your eyes again?
Have you closed your ears again?
Have you forgotten that day when your lives were threatened?

(Chorus) Have you forgotten? Stop the war! No more war again!

When the bullets crossed the air
When missiles cracked the soil
We must never fight again.
We must speak out now for love.
Let there be no tribalism,
That is why we bleed and die.
Freedom! Justice!
Freedom! Justice!
Love, Unity, Equality!

Above: Lagbaja plays sax in the destroyed high school at Wembezi, KwaZulu-Natal, South Africa, after hearing stories of daily political violence recounted by women in the township.

Right: Lagbaja plays his sax at an impromptu concert in Monrovia, Liberia, with the Don Bosco band, a group of former child soldiers and war orphans. In the background is John, the young bassist, who lost both legs in a massacre at St. Peter's church in downtown Monrovia which claimed the lives of 600 people, including his family.
Photographs by Paul Grabhorn

65

Love, Unity, Equality!
Where have they gone? They should've been here!
Violence can't be our way of speaking
Can't you see that no one else should live in fear! Aya!
Join your hands and speak for freedom.
Join your hands and speak for love.
You must be your brother's keeper.
Unity must be your goal
Look at what the past has been
Let it be a guide for us.

and *Drop Your Guns and Go to School*:

(Chorus) Drop your guns and go to school!
There is nothing in fighting wars!

They will tell you all about changes
But never hold an arm!
You will only kill your brothers
And make your mothers cry!
You should never kill a brother
Or make a sister cry!
Ah ya… Oh yo… woe… oh yo.

A deminer pulls the gasket to defuse a PMN2 anti-personnel mine in Huambo, Angola. An estimated 15 million landmines planted in Angola alone have maimed 70,000 Angolans to date. Buried but deadly, the mines deny farmers access to land, water and firewood.
Photograph by Paul Grabhorn

Danger! Mines! A sign marks a field full of landmines right beside a well-trodden path in Kuito, Angola. A team of British deminers working for Halo Trust is clearing the field, while villagers plant their crops just behind them.
Photograph by Paul Grabhorn

(Chorus)

Can't you hear your lovely mothers?
Crying "Come back home"!
Can't you see your lovely brothers?
Who are waiting to lend a hand!
Put away your weapons and let us go to School!
Ah ya… Oh yo… woe… oh yo.

(Chorus)

(Lyrics written and music composed by Peter Cole, Monrovia, Liberia.)

Six weeks later, the urban guerilla war resumed full-scale in the streets of Monrovia. Three thousand lost their lives. The Don Bosco Home was attacked and looted. John, Peter and Olas ran away and became refugees in Ivory Coast. Their musical instruments were either smashed or looted.

This was real preparation for the composition and recording of the song *So Why?* on Gorée Island in Senegal and the concert that followed in Paris.

---

11. Graça Machel, *The Machel Study – Impact of armed conflict on children.*
Submitted to the General Assembly of the United Nations, 26 August 1996, p.19

A huge fireball as Halo Trust detonates over a hundred unexploded rockets and anti-tank mines in Huambo, Angola. Some of the weapons being destroyed have been turned in by Government and opposition forces, others were found abandoned or planted in various locations around the city of Huambo.
**Photograph by
Paul Grabhorn**

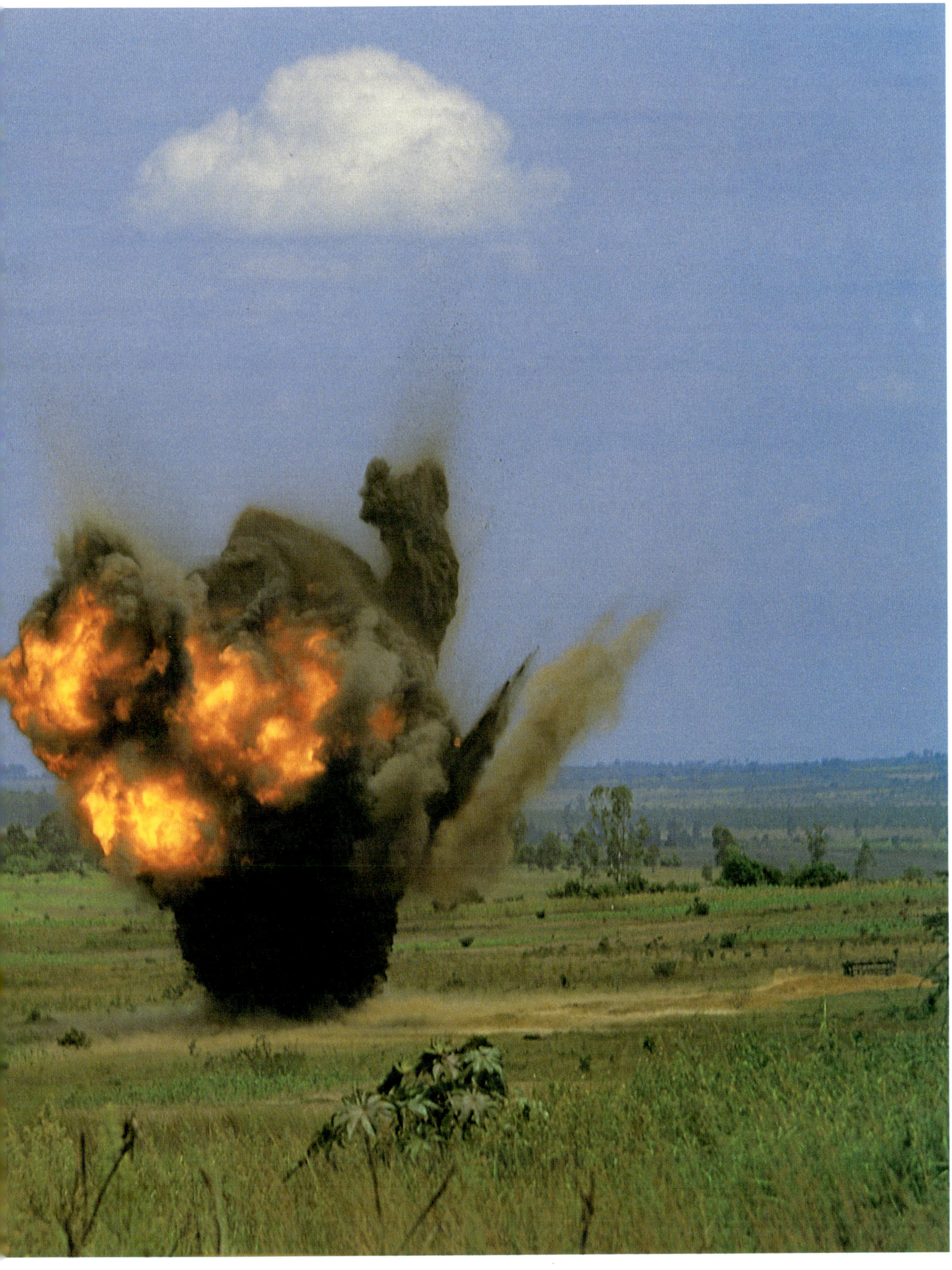

Angolan kids near a centre for children traumatized by war in Kuito. 8,000 children in Angola have been disabled by exploding mines, a deadly legacy of more than two decades of war.
**Photograph by Francesco Zizola,
World Press Photo of the Year, 1997**

What needs to be done

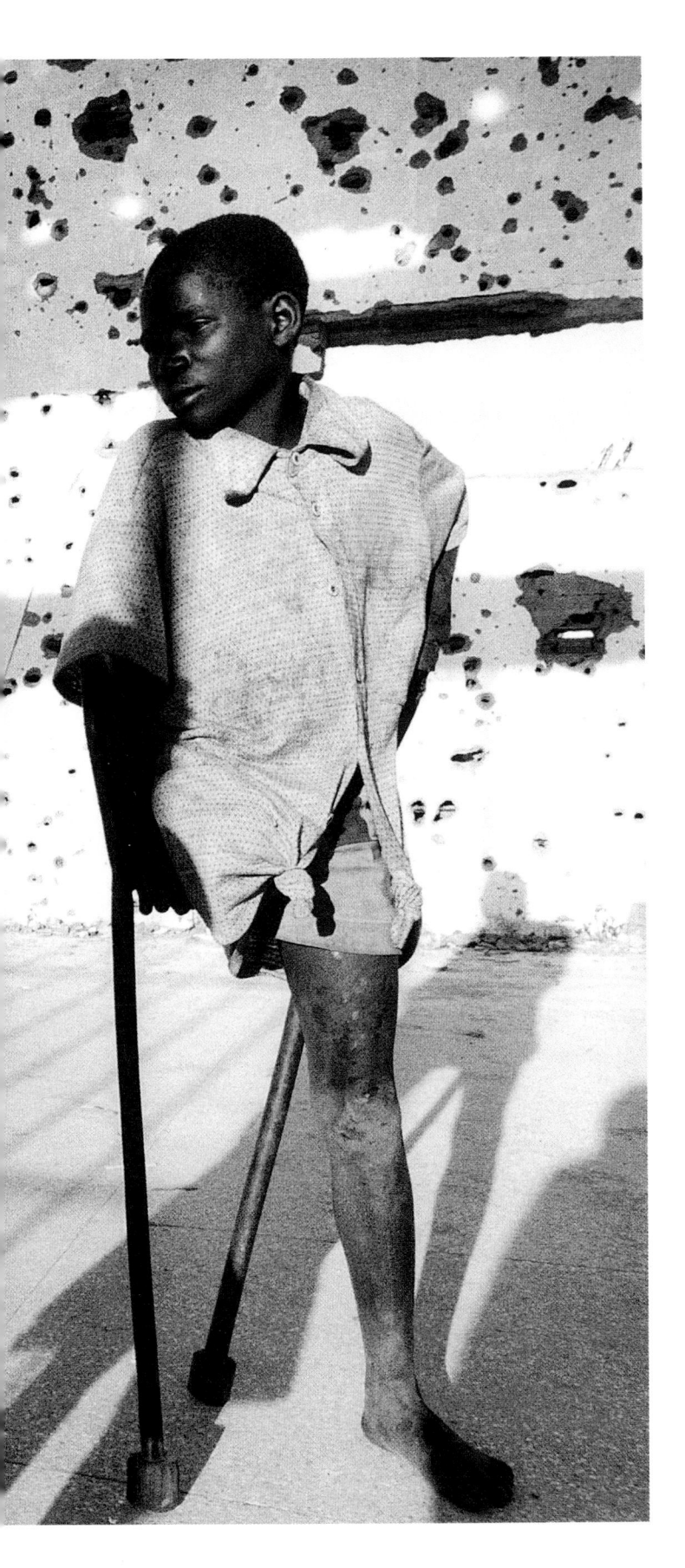

Given the past of slavery, colonization, exploitation and tribal antagonism in some African countries, war has been inevitable. The consequent division of Africa firstly into European zones of influence and then into designated states corraling multiple ethnic groups and languages within arbitrarily drawn boundaries could only lead to conflict. Two types of wars began to be waged in Africa – the war of liberation from colonial rule and the war of the struggle for power. The war of liberation from colonial rule seemed clear enough. Africans were fighting to regain control over their lands and their lives. The contending groups were clearly defined almost to the point of making the war a black and white issue. Almost as the wars of liberation were being terminated, the wars for power within the liberated states began. In some African states both wars went on at the same time, creating confusion and destroying the emergent state even before it could define itself. The breakdown of the state and the displacement of peoples, the landmines, the massacres and the general violence has led not only to human and material destruction but also to moral and cultural destabilization. The destruction of human lives has left everyone with a feeling that African lives are cheap. Material destruction makes construction of the necessary infrastructure for the renaissance of Africa impossible to put in place. Schools, hospitals, banks, cultural centres and roads are destroyed and reclaimed by the bush and forest. Farms and factories disappear and food shortage becomes the norm. During the wars of liberation, it was not unusual for the fighters to set up structures in the areas which they had recovered from the colonial powers with whom they were fighting. Ordinary civilians without any discrimination in terms of race, religion or ethnicity were considered to be the ultimate beneficiaries of the ensuing struggle. Unfortunately, wars involving power struggles tended to end as wars between ethnic groups. The carnage has been horrendous.

There is no doubt that the struggle is to control the state. But the state has to be created as a multi-ethnic state before it can be of use to anyone. If the state does not work for one person or one group, it cannot work for others, no matter who they are. The state is the instrument that Africans have not only to achieve the needed renovation of Africa but also to afford Africans participation in the society of states and be members of the international community. The state must therefore be secured, tended and grown.

There were wars in Africa before the historical encounter with Europe. There were wars in Europe before Europeans came to Africa. From the European experience has arisen the International Committee of the Red Cross with its concern for the victims of wars.

The International Committee of the Red Cross is the oldest independent humanitarian organization in the world. It has received a mandate from the international community to protect and assist victims of war and internal violence everywhere. Its activities in war zones are to visit and protect prisoners of wars and political detainees, to trace missing persons and reunite separated families, to care for the wounded and to reestablish water supplies, to provide displaced persons with food and vital relief as well as to distribute seeds and rehabilitation material.

Part of the mission statement of the International Committee of the Red Cross states:

> The ICRC's mission arises from the basic human desire, common to all civilizations, to lay down rules governing the use of force in war and to safeguard the dignity of the weak. The ICRC has received a mandate from the international community to help victims of war and internal violence and promote compliance with international humanitarian law. The ICRC has the duty to remind all States of their collective obligation to ensure respect for international humanitarian law.

If the state is the instrument through which the ICRC can achieve its aims and objectives, and the state ceases to exist because of war, as it did in Somalia and Liberia, for example, other ways are being explored to contin-

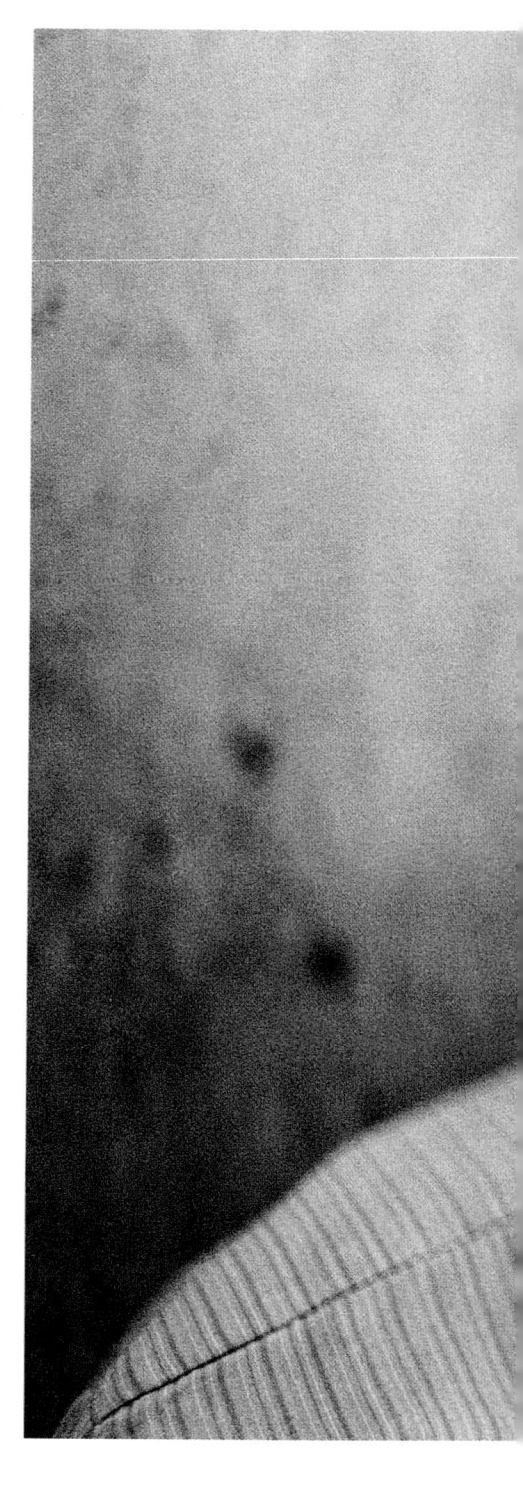

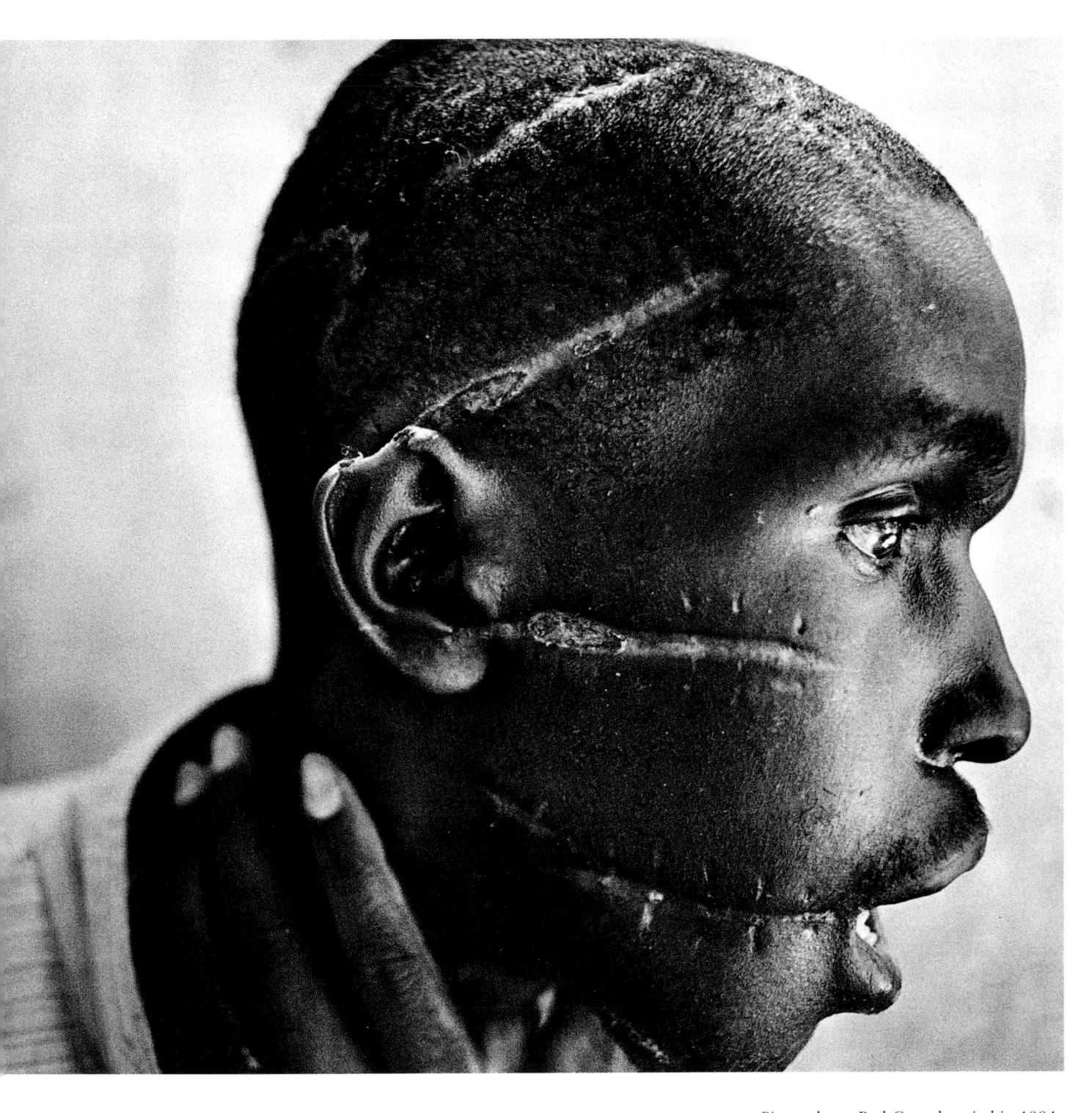

Pictured at a Red Cross hospital in 1994, this man is living proof of the atrocities perpetrated in Rwanda during the genocide. He has been mutilated with a machete by a militiaman.
**Photograph by James Nachtwey,
World Press Photo of the Year, 1995**

ue to operate in war zones and bring assistance and protection to the most needy. Special agreements are being negotiated with warlords or local authorities. This will not, however, replace proper implementation in the long term of laws and regulations protecting the most vulnerable in war time.

Africans are no strangers to war. But they had rules and regulations to govern such wars. The awareness of these traditional rules and regulations of war should make the intentions and the mission of the ICRC quite familiar to Africans. Again unfortunately, there has been an erosion of traditional morals of Africa and there has not been the entrenching of substitute morals.

Something needs to be done to correct this situation. On the legal level, there is need for the international community, the community of states which gave the ICRC its mandate, to ensure as a matter of priority that the rules and regulations governing warfare are implemented. If internationally accepted humanitarian laws were implemented or punishment followed refusal to implement them, a contribution would have been made towards the amelioration of the condition of the victims of warfare and political violence.

On the social level something must be done to revive those ancient African traditions which limit the use of violence. Such traditions must become an important component of the education of the African child.

These two suggestions depend on a third one: the personal element in warfare and political violence. There is a need for each of us to get involved as socially responsible individuals in "the modest morality of small deeds". This is not because we wish to prove how kind or public-spirited we are. More than this, it is like the moral: "if we do not do it for others now, nobody will be around to do it for us".

We are at our main meal of the day and debate circulates and cuts across plates of food and bottles of juice and other drinks. The question arises as

Left: A school in the village of Nyarubuye, where thousands of Tutsis were slaughtered in April 1994 and their corpses left to rot after the massacre, Rwanda, April 1995.
Photograph by Sebastião Salgado

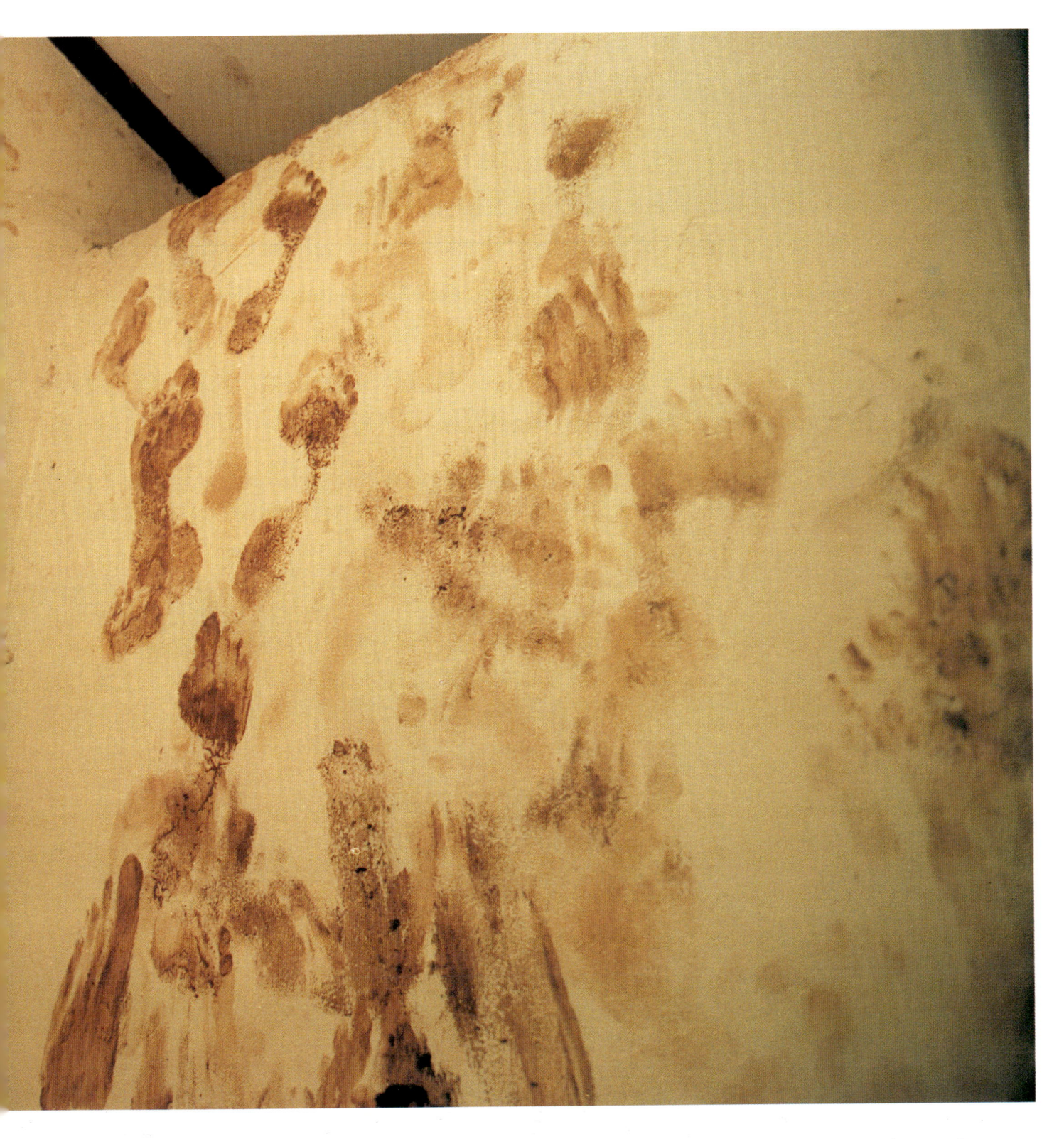

Above: Traces on the bathroom wall of a massacre of Tutsi schoolchildren and villagers at Shangi Mission School, south-western Rwanda, August 1994. Between 700,000 and one million Tutsis and moderate Hutus were massacred in Rwanda during the genocide.
Photograph by Annie Leibovitz

to what each of us would take if at that precise minute we have to leave our house of about six years and join tens of thousands of others in our area as refugees moving from Cape Town to Durban? Moji would take he cellular telephone, Picky could not decide immediately, Boney would take a warm jacket, a basketball and his CD walkman, Doucee would take her diary and I opted to take my Yoruba language Bible. Of what use would these things be to us on that long march to Durban or anywhere else? And when confronted with such sudden departures in desperate situations, do we think of the past or of the future in choosing what to bring with us?

Construction of a hospital for a refugee camp in the village of Niocuche, southern Sudan, 1995.
Photograph by Sebastião Salgado

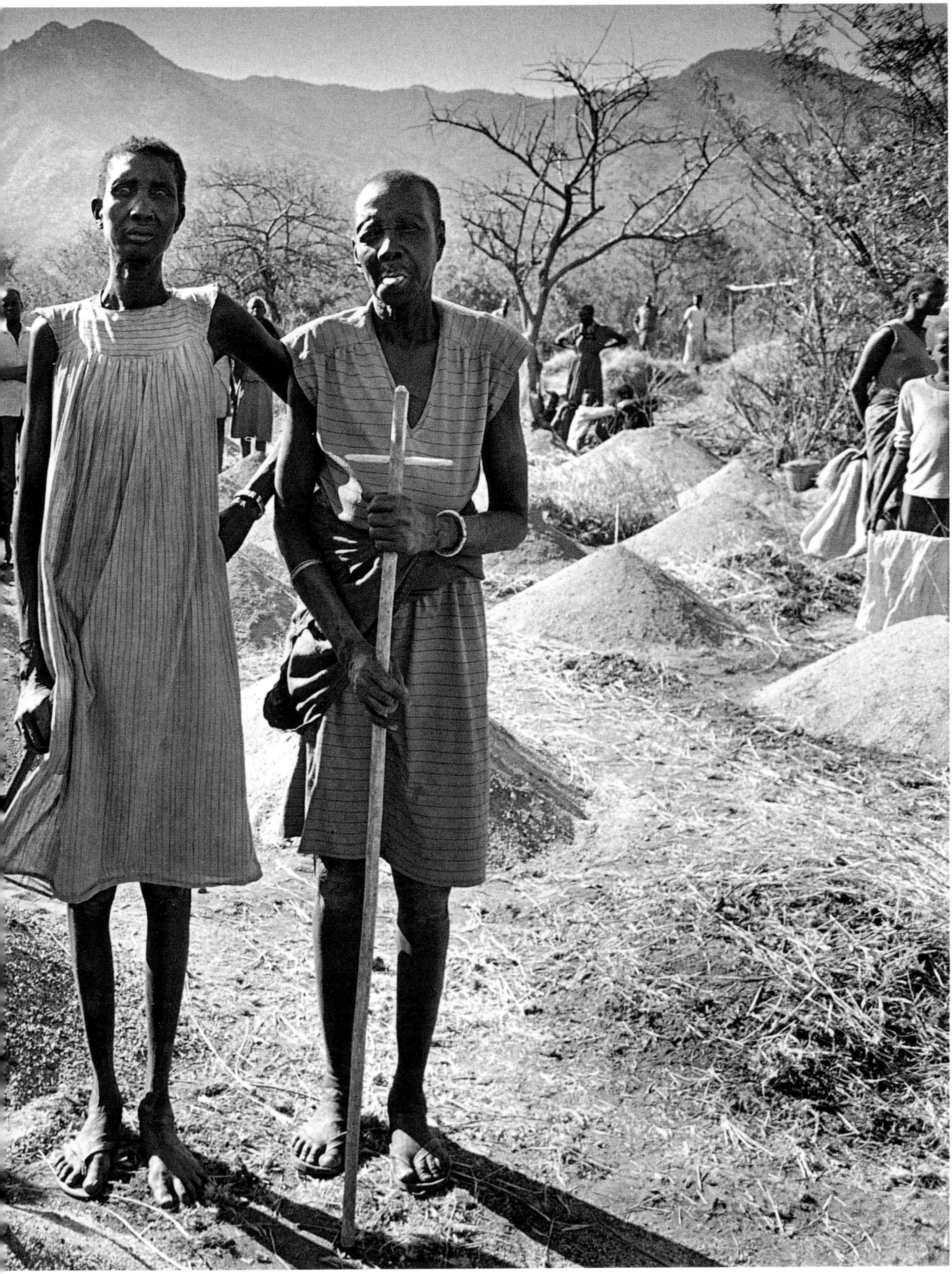

A few days after this I watched a video documentary of middle-class professional Africans forced to flee their houses and become refugees. What many carried with them were the choicest items of contemporary consumerism – a cassette recorder, foam mattresses, electric lawnmowers, two servants! In an eighteen-kilometre-long refugee column numbering over a quarter of a million people – men, women, children – moving within a time span of forty-eight hours, these possessions are soon discarded for the most basic need – a container, preferably plastic, with which to obtain water.

President Nelson Mandela has spoken out for the renaissance of Africa. In practical terms this means that, besides developing democracy and increasing respect for human rights, Africa must modernize and become part of the international community. This also means that Africa's resources must be converted to financial resources. The main reason that ordinary civilians suffer in these wars is that while they are money-poor, they arc resources-rich. Because the state is not strong enough yet to monetarize these resources, ordinary civilians lose out. They have no money and their resources of land, water and lives are destroyed or else gravely threatened.

The process of renaissance is not easy. The present wars must be seen as the birth throes of the process. Looked at in this way, wars are not a permanent condition.

Yet, many African states are facing great structural problems. Unlike the European state on which it was modelled, distinct ruling elites and classes have not emerged. What exists is a multiplicity of individuals from differing ethnic groups and languages. Many of these could have been antagonists in time past. Such antagonisms could have been made worse by the colonial experience. The new African state needs to be established, nurtured and grown and must of necessity be multi-ethnic, multi-lingual and multi-religious. There is no longer a place for a state that is of one ethnic origin, speaks one language and worships one common deity. Each ethnic, linguistic and religious group brings into the new African configuration values from its pre-colonial past which contribute to the totality of the values of the new state. Besides contributing to the new vision, each group also benefits equally without any prejudice whatever. It is only the emergence of such a state that can take steps to ensure the re-establishment of the implementation of humanitarian laws, the reviving of ancient African traditions and the inclusion of such traditions in the education of the African child. Over and above everything, it is within such a state that individuals would feel committed enough to their own future to care for the future of their neighbours, their communities as well as the state itself. Such a state would then be in a position to be part of the international community that accepts responsibility and implements its legal obligations under the Geneva Conventions and International Humanitarian Law. It is to this end that the international community must assist Africans to grow their states and make them the instruments of their renaissance.

There have always been civil societies in African communities. There were economic societies pooling resources which were allocated to individual members of the society at different times. There were artistic societies

A child in the Mekele refugee camp at the time of famine, Tigray, Ethiopia, 1984.
Photograph by David Burnett

An overcrowded prison where most of the many thousands of prisoners are Hutus suspected of having taken part in the genocide, Kigali, Rwanda, 1995.
Photograph by Sebastião Salgado

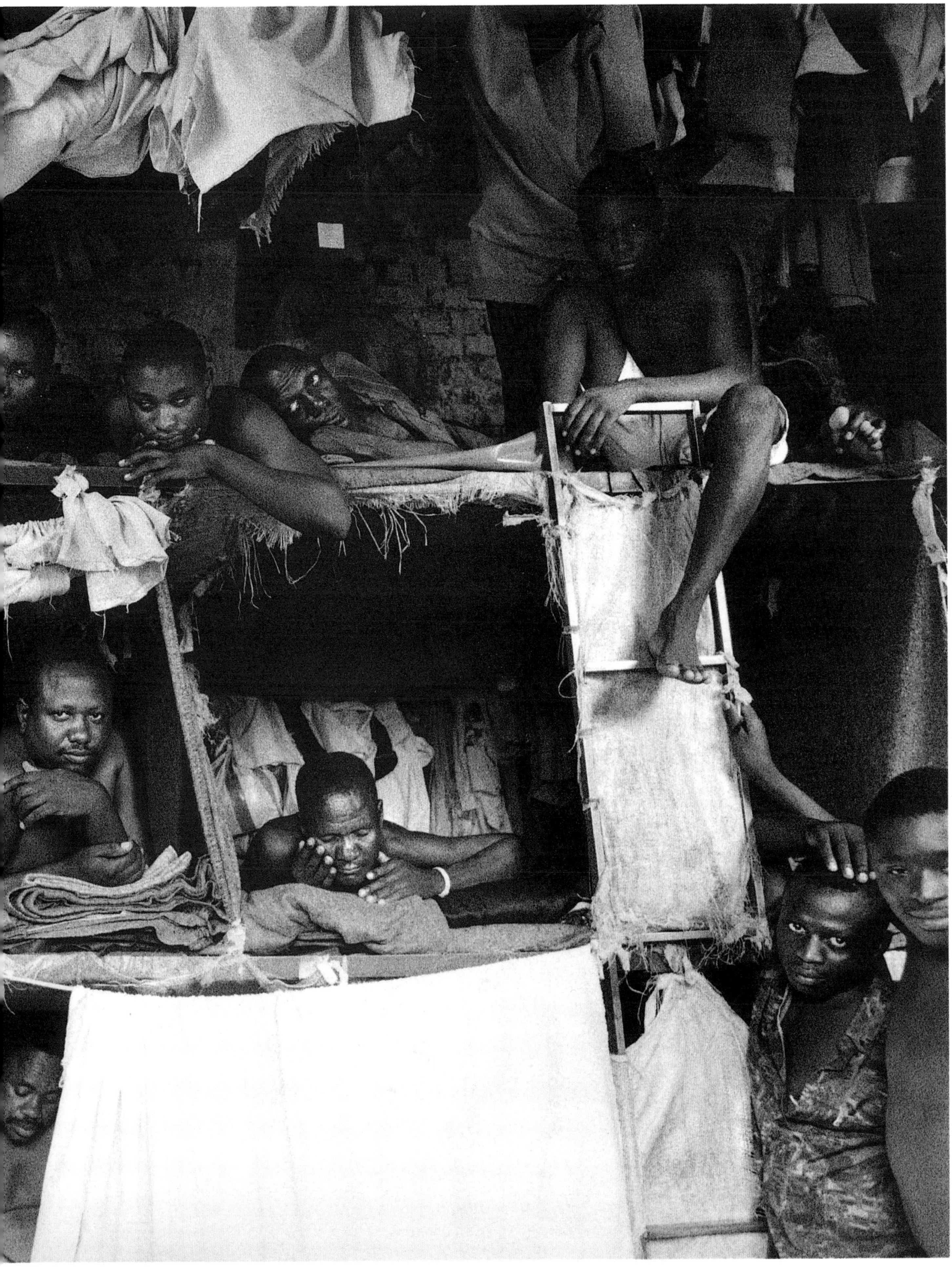

of carvers, drummers, blacksmiths creating together and aiding one another to create as individuals. There were professional societies of women and men mastering their professions as market women and men, fish-sellers or farmers. These different civil societies have a responsibility to themselves and the rest of the community to ensure that no part of the community harms the communal health. Operating in the modern mode of non-governmental organizations, they can contribute towards the stabilization of the state and the survival of its infrastructures. Through the combination of a multi-ethnic state and a variety of civil societies, it would be apparent that what the state unites is not cultures and languages since it is not the unity of cultures that is the objective but rather that the state should unite the common vision of a modernized community.

The roles of the state and the civil societies are important but the most important role in the re-creating of African morals and cultures is that of the individual. Individuals must accept and practise the "modest morality of small deeds" by caring for one another, by being their brothers' and sisters' keepers.

In wars, because of the volume of people moving from one place to another and across international boundaries, children get abandoned.

Sometimes the string which an elder child ties around a younger sibling breaks and the child is lost. Then the ache of waiting starts and for the parents a deep anxiety of not knowing the child's whereabouts. It sometimes takes years to trace lost children and when a child is finally reunited with

Above: a rally for international aid during famine and civil war, Mogadishu, Somalia, 1992.
Photograph by Alexandra Avakian

Right: a hospital filled with refugees driven out from their homes as a result of military activity, Labone, southern Sudan, 1995.
Photograph by Sebastião Salgado

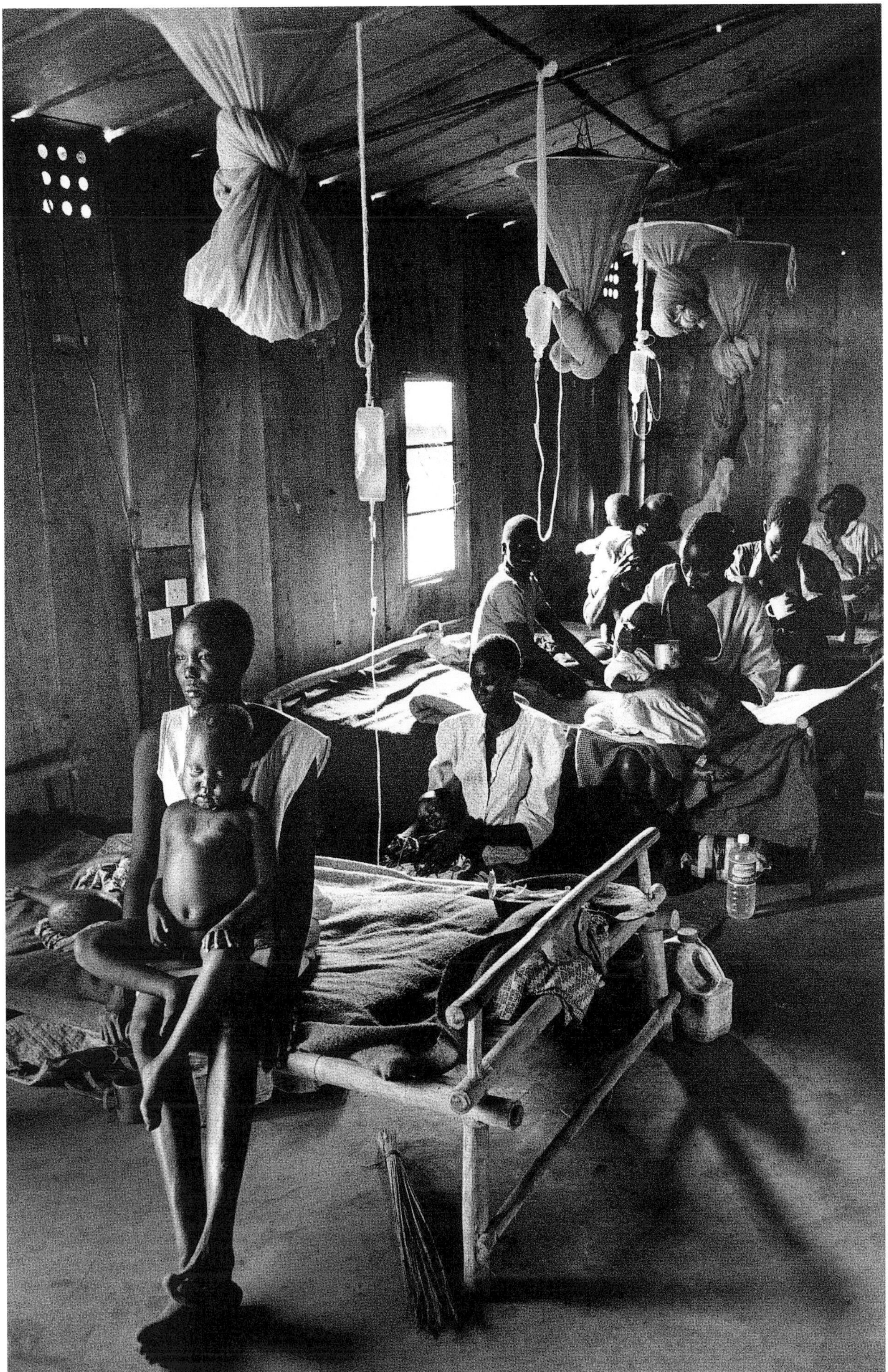

A general view of Kibeho refugee camp, the largest in south-western Rwanda, March 1995. A month after this picture was taken, the camp was attacked and a large number of refugees were massacred. **Photograph by Sebastião Salgado**

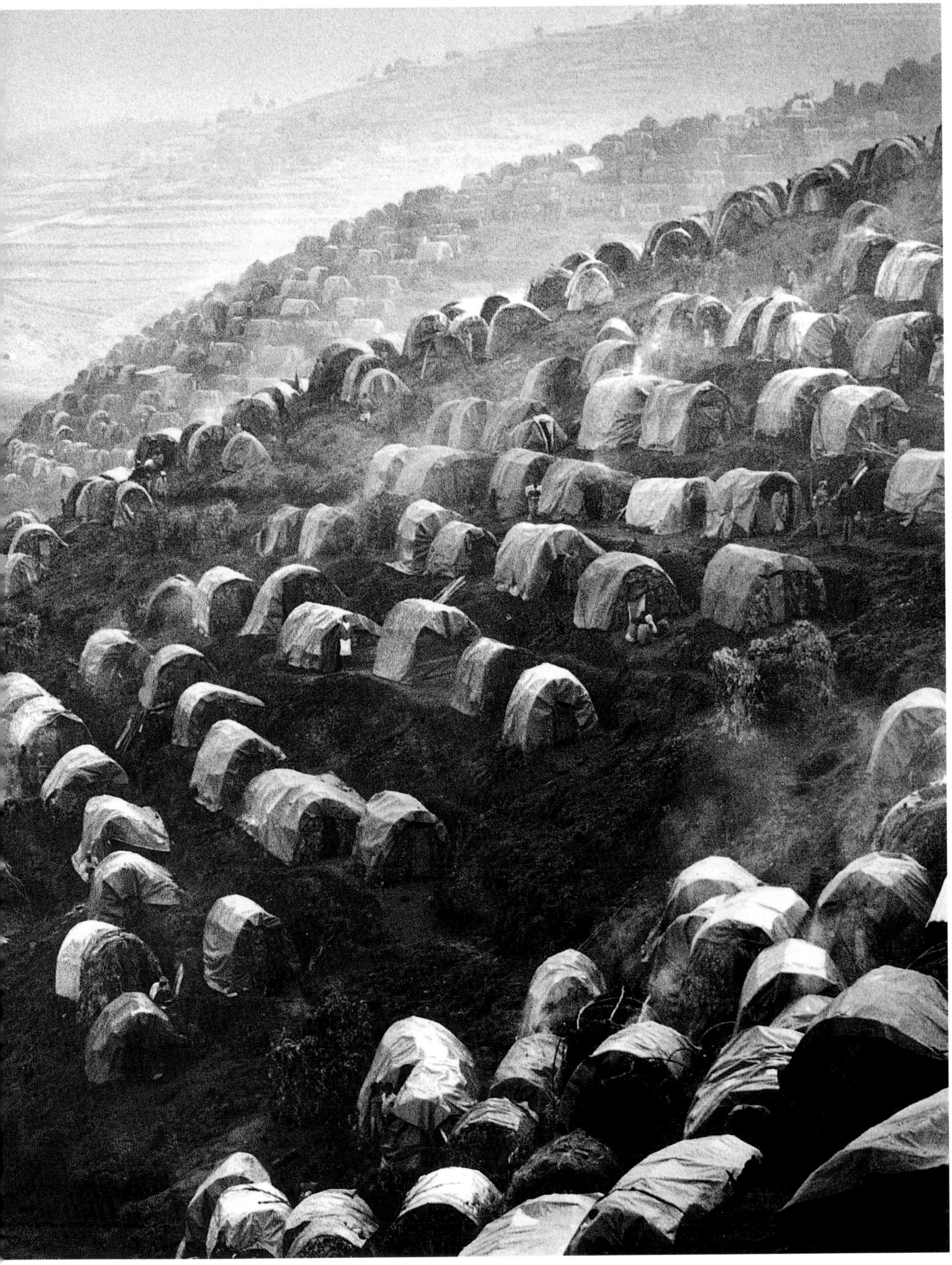

his mother these final steps are magical.

Just as war is not a permanent condition, the enmity which it engenders cannot be permanent. Thus, the embrace of reconciliation is more welcome today in Africa than ever before. So, why then do we endure these wars and violence and chaos?

Listen to our musicians ask *So Why?*

Papa Wemba (*presenting the song*)
This song is
All emotion
All sorrow.
It is a cry for us Africans
To put an end to killing one another.
The new generation must understand
That tribalism combined with hatred spells war.
But war is not inevitable
Our ethnic differences
Constitute the wealth of Africa
On condition
That all of us Africans learn to live together!
For me, this trip has changed forever how I look at Africa and I will tell my children!

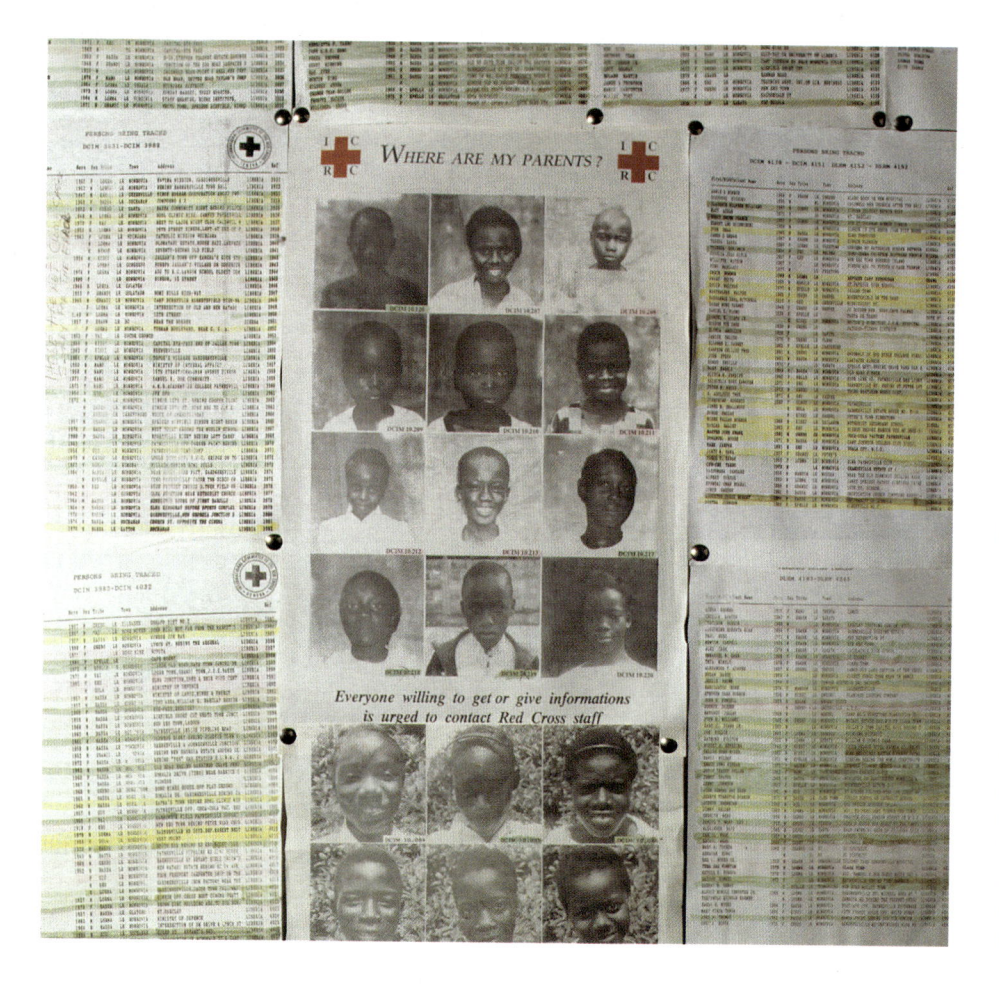

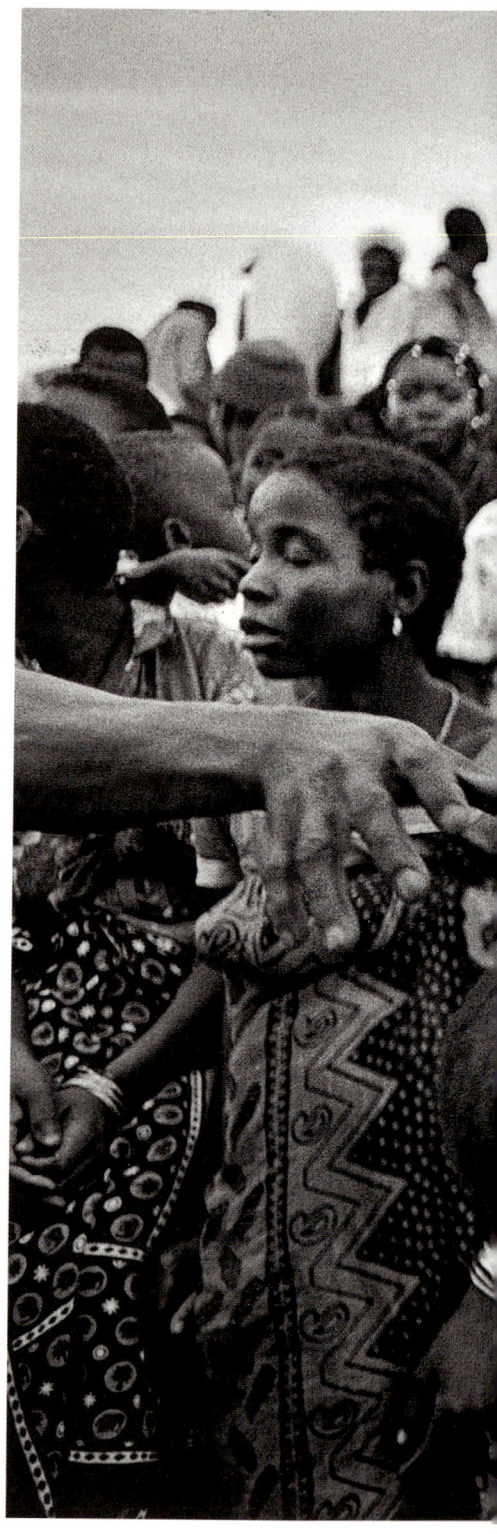

Left: in war, children lose their way. ICRC tracing board with lists and photographs of lost children, Monrovia, Liberia, 1992. When more than a million people fled Rwanda during the genocide in 1994, 90,000 children were separated from their parents. Between 1994 and 1997, thanks to the ICRC central database in Nairobi, the Red Cross, Unicef, Save the Children and other aid organizations have been able to reunite 38,259 children with their families.
Photograph by Luc Chessex

Above: the crossing of Lake Niassa during the repatriation of refugees from Tanzania to Mozambique after the restoration of peace, July 1994.
Photograph by Sebastião Salgado

A man whose hands were cut off by a militiaman recovers in hospital, Rwanda, July 1994.
Photograph by Corinne Dufka

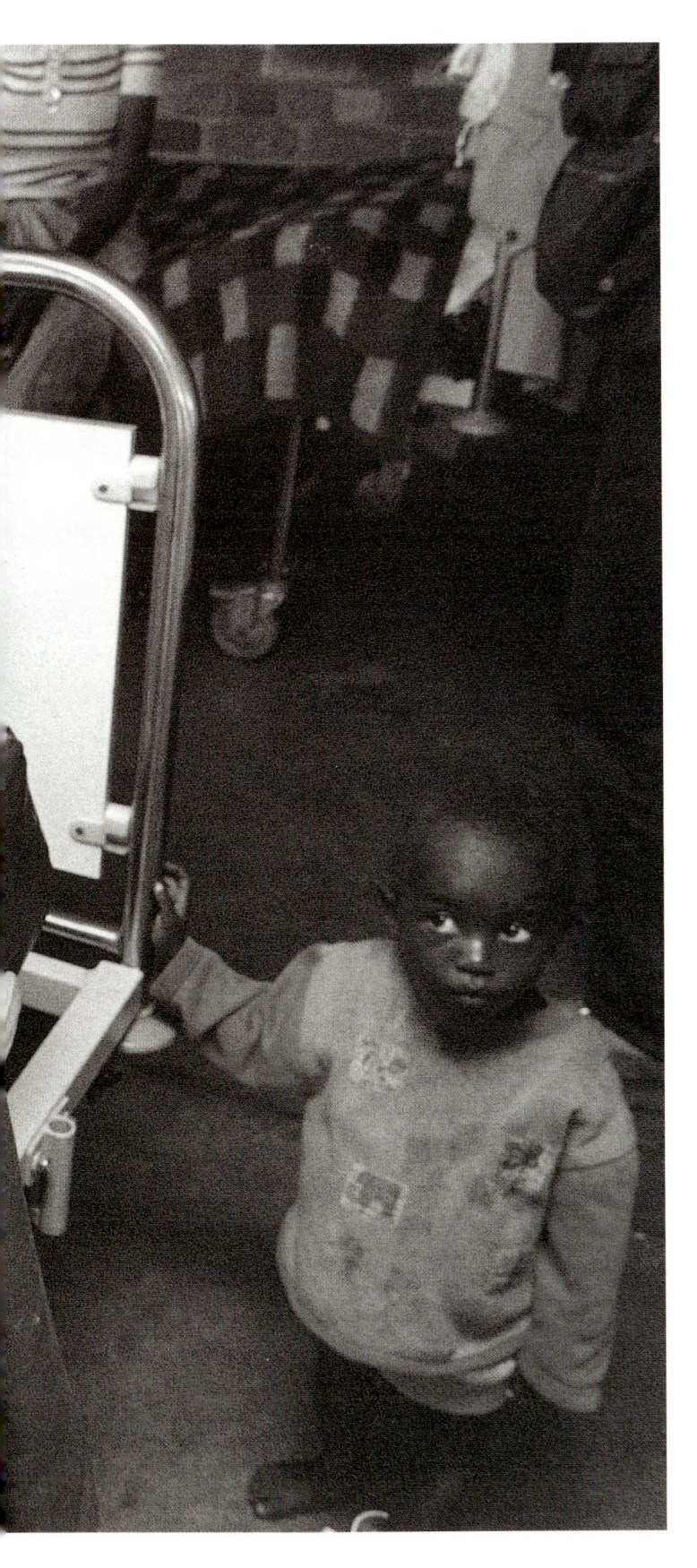

So Why?

Music by Wally Badarou. Original lyrics in ten African languages. Released in October 1997.

Jabu Khanyile of Bayete

I've been asking for peace
But all I got was war
I've been looking for love
But I didn't find togetherness
What is wrong with the world
What is wrong with the people?
Why don't we want peace?

Papa Wemba

Terrible things are happening in Africa
All that we see in Africa, oh my God
Mother nourisher wake up
Mother look to the skies, things are about to change
I see angels dressed in white making music
Motherland give me sustenance
Motherland, teach me
Motherland, take note of the tears of your children

(Refrain)
Africa, Africa will sing – So Why?
My people, your people are key – So Why?
Together, united, we can stand – So Why?

Lourdes Van-Dunem

Whether you are from Rwanda, Angola, Senegal, Zaire
  or South Africa is not important.
What is important is that we are all Africans.
Whether black or white is not important.
What is crucial is that we respect each other!

Youssou N'Dour

Remember always that man is a remedy to man
  – Wake up!
Why war, why this, why, why, why war ooh?
Victims of war, why so much hatred?
Deported, forgotten, wo, wo, wo, woo
We have to forgive. My generation.
Let there be another generation
How could you justify what happened before?

Lagbaja

My people. Oh Africa,
Wak... wak... wak... Wake up! Wak... wak...
Wake up Africa!
Cool your anger. Tolerate each other
Please, please
Please... oh please
Together, united, we can stand, So Why?
Wak... wak... wak... wak... Wake up! Wak...
  wak... wak...
Wake up Africa!

(Refrain)
Africa, Africa will sing – So Why?
My people, your people are key – So Why?
Together, united, we can stand – So Why?
Tears, my tears!
Africa, Africa will sing – So Why?
The sun in your heart is your smile – So Why?
Come on, let's call for peace – So Why?

Jabu Khanyile of Bayete

Says the skeleton of Africa
Africa, the world is rotting
People are turning to evil
The world is rotting
The world is wounded
Sudan, Rwanda, Angola, Malawi, Liberia, Zaire
Stop the killing
Stop the killing
South Africa: war is never good.
Stop the killing
Reconciliation is the key road
Ho Africa! Ho Africa!
Let's move forward!

Youssou N'Dour

Children of Africa,
We all share the same values
Is there any goal better than that?
We must never forget what is happening today

(Refrain)
So Why?
So Why?
So Why?
Africa, Africa will sing – So Why?

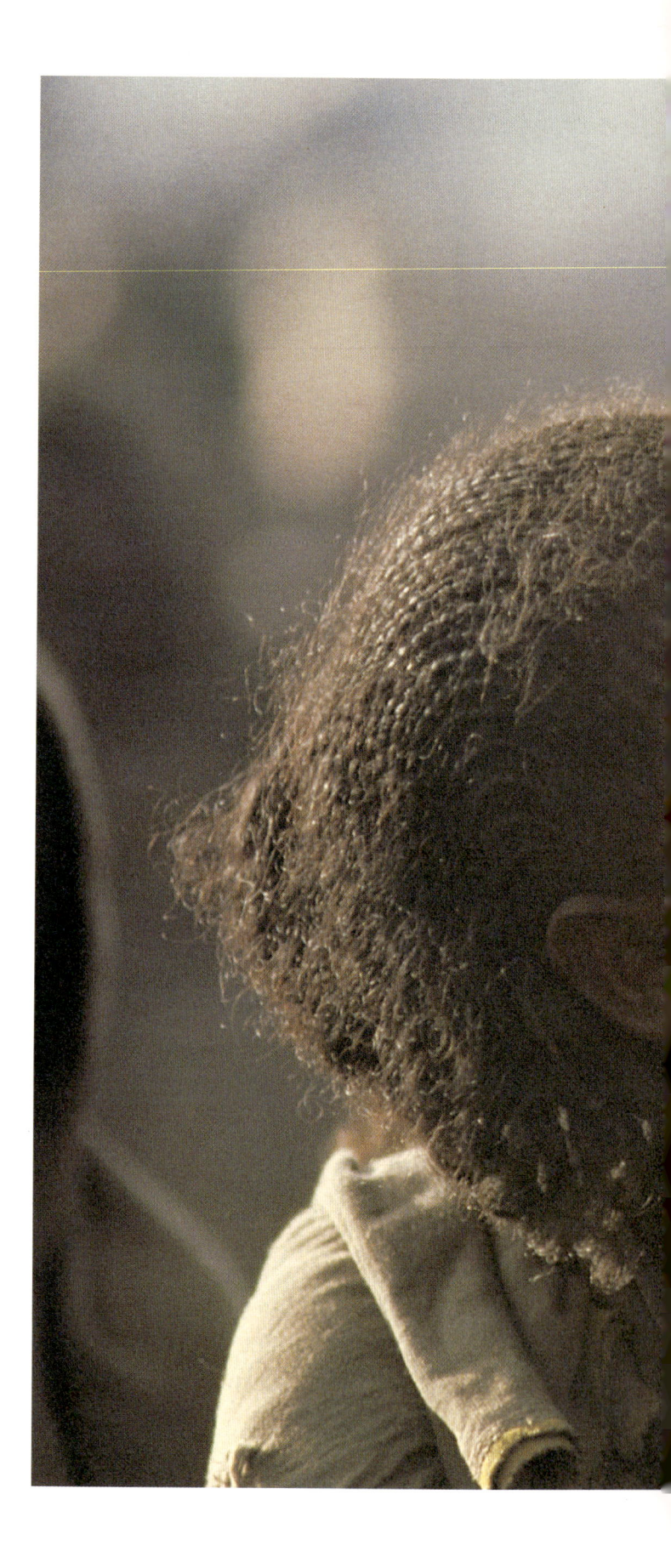

A mother and child in the Korem refugee camp during the great famine, Wollo, Ethiopia, 1984.
Photograph by David Burnett

The sun in your heart is your smile – So Why?
Come on, let's call for peace – So Why?

Lagbaja
Sierra Leone
Angola, Algeria, Somalia, Liberia, Nigeria, Rwanda
Zaire, Burundi, Sudan, wake up!

Papa Wemba
The Life of our children has no more meaning.

Lagbaja
For the sake of tomorrow
Stop the war, stop the destruction
We've got to stop this barbarism in the name of tribalism!

(Refrain)
My people, your people are key – So Why?
Together, united, we can stand – So Why?
Africa, Africa will sing – So Why?
My people, your people are key – So Why?
Together, united, we can stand – So Why?

Lourdes Van-Dunem
We are one people
My people united
United for Africa
Together for ever
For peace and love
For ever for Africa

Youssou N'Dour
New generation
Why love, why war, why, why?
Why war, why this, why no love?
New generation
Oh, so why love, why no love?
Sooo Why, Sooo Why?

(Refrain)
Tears, my tears
Africa, Africa will sing – So Why?
The sun in your heart is your smile – So Why?
Come on, let's call for peace – So Why?

Boys play in water coming from a tanker truck which got stuck while delivering life-giving clean water to refugees displaced by fighting. The exuberance of youth in a war zone, Gihanga region, Burundi, 1995.
Photograph by Paul Grabhorn

Children born in foreign countries see their homeland for the first time after returning from a Malawian refugee camp. Mutarara, Mozambique, 1994. **Photograph by Sebastião Salgado**

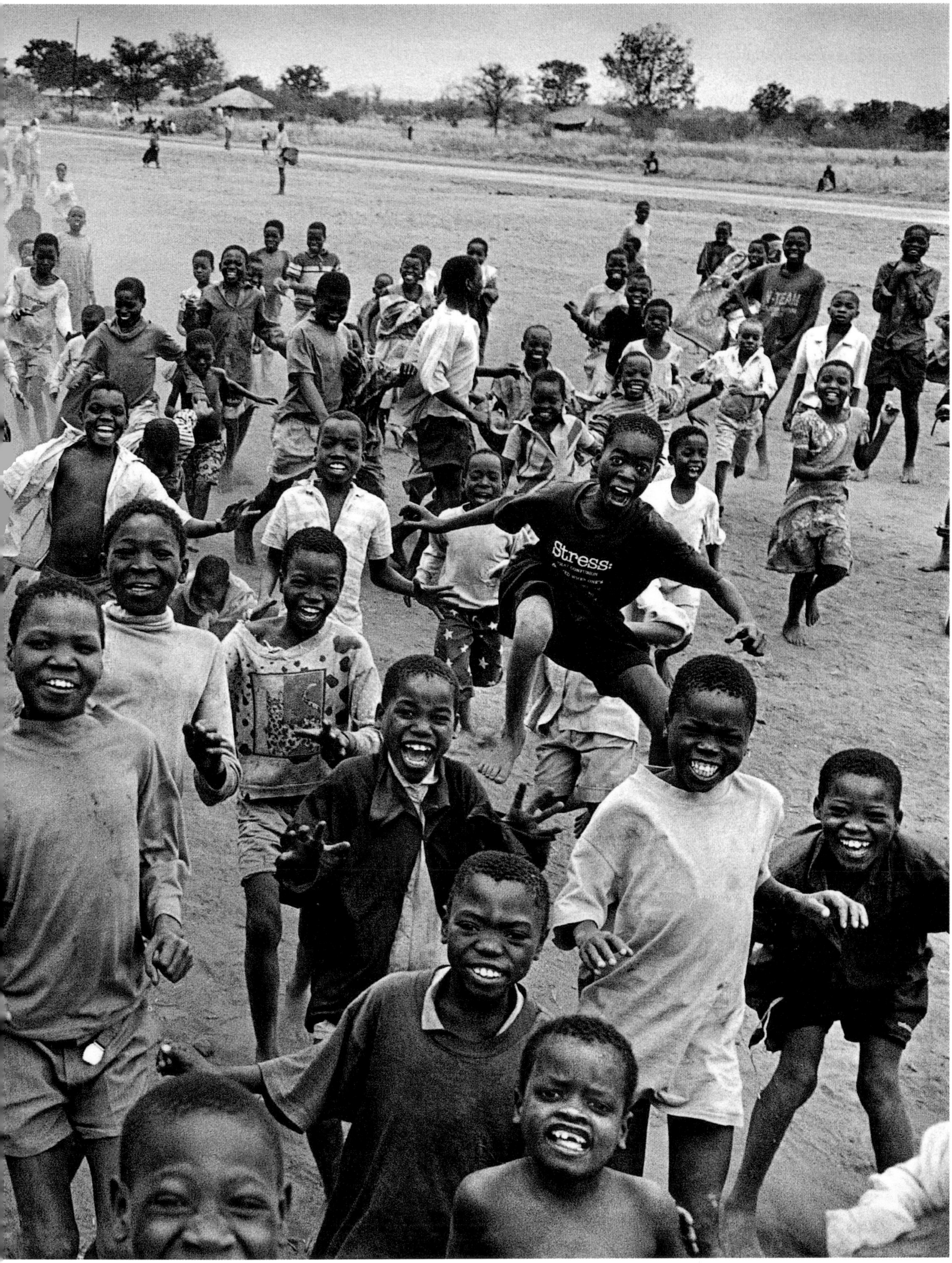
Stress:

Acknowledgements

The International Committee of the Red Cross (ICRC)
wishes to express its gratitude to the following persons and organizations
whose generous contributions made this book possible:

Youssou N'Dour, Dakar.
Papa Wemba, Paris.
Lagbaja, Lagos.
Jabu Khanyile, Soweto.
Lucky Dube, Johannesburg.
Lourdes Van-Dunem, Luanda.
Wally Badarou, Paris.

Douglas and Françoise Kirkland with Scott Browning, Los Angeles.
Paul Grabhorn, Washington DC.

Kole Omotoso and his family, Cape Town.

President Nelson Mandela, Pretoria.

Robert Y. Pledge, Co-Founder and President of Contact Press Images, Paris.
*Photos: pp.6, 28–29, 31, 32–33, 36–37, 38, 39, 40–41, 42–43,
74, 75, 76–77, 78–79, 80–81, 82, 83, 84–85, 86–87, 90–91, 94–95.*
Magnum Photos, London. *Photos: pp.24–25, 26–27, 72–73.*
Reuters, Nairobi. *Photos: pp.34–35, 88–89.*
Katz Pictures, London. *Photo: pp. 48–49.*
Agenzia Contrasto, Milan. *Photo: pp.70–71.*
Network Photographers, London.
World Press Photo, Amsterdam.
And all the great photographers who freely contributed to this book:
James Nachtwey, Sebastião Salgado, Corinne Dufka, Alexandra Avakian, David Burnett,
Gilles Caron, Jean-Claude Coutausse, Annie Leibovitz,
Tomas Muscionico, Francesco Zizola, Guenay Ulutunçok, Luc Chessex, Rodger Bosch.

Yolande Bacot and the staff of "Le Parc de la Villette", Paris.

ICRC staff in Durban, Pretoria, Nairobi, Lokichokio, Kigali, Luanda,
Huambo, Kuito, Monrovia, Abidjan, Dakar, Lagos, Kinshasa and Geneva.

All together, more than 150 great people without whom this book would not exist.